My Hospitals & My Prisons

PAUL VERLAINE
"The Prince of Poets"

Translated By Richard Robinson

Sunny Lou Publishing Company
Portland, Oregon, USA
http://www.sunnyloupublishing.com

2nd edition: January 9, 2024
1st edition corrected: November 25, 2021
Original publication date: July 23, 2020

ISBN: 978-1-955392-50-1

* * *

This translation from French is based on the
Librairie Léon Vanier, Publisher, 4th tome, 3rd
edition of *ŒUVRES COMPLÈTES de PAUL
VERLAINE*, Paris, 1909.

Contents

My Hospitals

I

At least this wasn't the fault of literature, which would have showered him with gold and honors, but quite a bit his own fault and that of another, isn't that right, dear Madam? – if he found himself in the hospital. Without insisting on this point any longer, however insignificant, I'm not the one who will speak, it's he who will speak, and that, rather impersonally, according to his particular temperament as a poet.

In the high-ceiling wards of a literal palace, weeks of apprenticeship passed. The immense white curtains in front of the windows, and the beautiful July sun filled his soul with a warm freshness which some ready cash secured for him and which would run out eventually, such that his current situation, on the spot and outside, didn't seem painful, him being, at the most, proud of his minor difficulties. The head doctors and their internal and external staff, – what else is there to say but that they were quite good; the employees also (the Church calls them *servants*) and some patients, except for the poor folk who did their best to get better. One death only in these forty some odd days, an old man who passed away while mumbling: "Mama, mama!" In sum, a very good first impression, a courageous debut, but easy...

Less easy, if not less courageous the second hardship experienced. The rough and hard, but seemingly protective, palace, modeled, it seems, on American flying ambulances, was succeeded by barracks

made of fir and brick. The exterior resembled passably some slaughterhouse, inside of which is the architecture of a Methodist chapel; the only thing missing are quotes by Saint Paul on white varnished
boards hung on the wall. One might also say the re-
union hall of some newly installed seaside health resort.

It is two days after All Saints. The windows
look out over a florist-horticulturalist's garden, lying
next to the railway belt. A row of black locust trees
makes up the edge of a wood the interior of whose
fortifications seen from behind would constitute
thickness; but the leaves, thinning, quickly defeat this
optical illusion. The doctors and students are always
perfect, but at the same time appear a little too skeptical and conceited; the personnel, my God, always irreproachable, but the patients do not seem crazy
about the departure of the Sisters. The latter are crab-
by and some of them uglier than is right. Around two
o'clock, the night assistant arranges, on a large central
buffet called the *apparatus*, pewter pots for herbal
tea. A drawsheet (or half-sheet), which he will cover
them with during the sweeping, looks like, after he
threw it over his shoulders from which it hangs down
around his body and along his arms, the surplice of a
priest arranging lots of Holy Oils: the wadding, in
tufts and flocks, here and there, completes the image.

Deep sleeps sometimes. One is awakened at
dawn to "make your bed." The chambermaid is from
the countryside, recently gotten off the train, practically the stagecoach. A somewhat simple girl without
too much naïvety and very good really. No shadow of
a thought of personal interest. She goes about it so
kindly to tell you: "Lazy bones, get out of bed now,
so I may freshen up your pillows," that one is com-

pletely charmed and unable to hold back the least sensual smile, for she is young still and has a pleasant face.

Hardly an incident happened over the course of a semester in winter, amidst the suffocating heat of smoke from the coke in the cast-iron heater. An alcoholic, – a pig! – very reasonable during the day, escapes one morning at about 4 o'clock and leaps half-naked out from one of the windows, from the ground floor, some fifty centimeters approximately, and returns on a stretcher, having been arrested at the city gates, with this on his lips: "But it's not me, I assure you." All that's needed is a glacial moonlight, cutting objects in two like a pair of scissors, falsifying every perspective, a dubious sun with its mad rays, and it is very Thessalian and very Canidian.

Insignificant deaths. And then one gets used to it. A darkened pecuniary situation that grows obscure.

An entr'acte absolutely black: Poverty and nearly the rope, so much so that a recrudescence of the malady and admittance to a third hospital are welcome events. At least it is peaceful being far from people and left alone with one's suffering. Ideas of death, death of people, death of oneself, evaporate amongst the odors of ether and phenol. The blood beats more calmly, the mind reasons again, the hands become what they rather always were, good and peaceful. As well the place grows comfortable with the appeasement that it creates, end of the eighteenth century in arrangement, and Louis-Philippe and the year 1848 in accommodation. The interior of the building has above all the feeling of those country houses with very high ceilings. The parquet, waxed to the extreme, sometimes bulging with old age, bespeaks, by its disposition, in fantastic chamfered edges, the considerable age of this lodging. It's in a little room set off from another one that is much longer, behind an insulating revolving glass door without isolating the rest of the patients who are four in number. That creates a room taking its light largely from a relatively unfrequented suburb on the left bank, facing a light-green garden of a superior educational establishment of the State. We're in spring and there are birds.

The intensity of the situation at the same time desperate and to be salvaged by patience when everything tends toward superb acts of violence that would ruin things frightfully, puts a bandage over one's eyes and wax in one's ears. Without a doubt, the uninteresting ugliness and the stupidities that banality renders more horrible still, disappear. An odiously modern chapel where, however, a pretty voice sings over a quiet harmonium. Because the women wear a horrid outfit, one sees nothing of patients belonging to the "finer sex," with the exception of two or three old women and all the reedy girls made eyes at already, for the most part.

Appears that in the back, to the left of the delivery pavilion, are barracks just like over there. Thanks. Been there done that.

Gas, in the definitive hospital, is contained to its proper role as a domestic. It lights up the kitchens, offices, corridors, stairs, – and loos.

Difinitif is used here because one aspires to no longer frequent those sorts of asylums, even if it means getting into worse shelters if bad luck proves stubborn also.

II

There, there, everything is fine, Mr. Poet. Life is not so short as all that, nor so brief. It is made of transitions. Patience has its role to play which is prepotent. On the other hand, the determining causes[1] of your introduction into hospitals have not disappeared, far from it. Finally, the vow to get familiar with other shelters was not reasonable and is found perhaps too ambitious in the present case. You have understood and you have resigned yourself to the inevitable. New impressions await you in the same milieux, and if there must be a different end than the natural end for those habits of an ascetic somewhat in spite of himself, nobody knows it. There always exists a sequel, witness whereof some fragments that follow and which behold! have become succinct.

The word convalescence was mentioned, and it is now a central pavilion, a diminutive and simplified version of the Tuileries' central pavilion, but given the Napoleonic touch of a vast imperial escutcheon at the front of it: the eagle in repose on lightning bolts and, behind, in drapery, the large coat sown with bees, stuffed with ermine, that a necklace of miniscule eagles borders whence hangs a large cross of honor, all in stone, naturally. Heavy and banal and ugly enough, in parenthesis, as might be said without showing any disrespect to the

"Deceased Caesar."

To the right and to the left, a ground floor and a floor with high glass windows and, at right angles,

---

[1]determining causes: presumably alcoholism and the effects of it.

two wings, stone, brick, and wood, suggestive of immense outhouses, stables, and sheds that never end,
the entirety a bit grandiose with four large, little gardens around a rather vast basin and, front and center,
an enormous lawn dotted here and there by rather
poorly flowering baskets, but wasn't the palace intended for the poor and must one forget it?

The buildings are snuggled very deeply in the
form of rather low lateral galleries such that the eye
can discern, light and clear, the gentle trees of a ple-
beian wood in the immediate environs of Paris, in the
middle of which, moreover, as if in a clearing, these
constructions rise up agreeable after all.

It's Napoleon III, the Well-Intentioned, who
founded this asylum for the hospitals' convalescents.
The very disposition of the interiors, the very character of the house's usages and customs, proclaim to the
degree of excess that source: the long barrack-like
wards, divided into rooms with three beds, which recall the *small rooms* of hospitals, and a discipline a
little like that of prison; the refectories with red mar-
ble tables, with small cast-iron columns gaily varnished, bringing back memories of the first manifestations of Bouillons Duval, that creation of the second
imperial epoch at its apogee; the names, for the most
part Swiss, of the galleries, wards, and dormitories,
sound good in an institution founded by good ole
General Dufour's favorite pupil: finally the regulations, evident work of the philanthropist tainted by
Fourierism who was the conqueror of Saarebruck,
those regulations recited and recited again on all occasions by the monitors, I was going to say by the
guards, with gray mustaches redolent of ex-grenadiers
of Magenta, with medals from Mexico and China, – it
all smells a lot like the prisoner of Ham not without

some odor of atavistic militarism.

To accompany the "panem" of the refectories, there is nothing until the "circences"[2] of the singing rooms and game rooms (games in wood: chess, checkers, dominos or, better yet, *doches)* which hardly suggest, from the decadent point of view, what the rhetoric, still employed by one-sou journals, would call the "disastrous gifts of a dictatorship fortunately pulverized under the national rebuilding."

We'll come back in a moment to the singing room. The game room is, as is the singing room besides, a vast parallelogram furnished with long tables and benches, where one smokes while advancing to a queen or crowning a double-*doche*.

But, between the two refectories, concealed behind ample draperies of somber red fabric, there is principally the chapel that screams the son of Hortense and his reign, while the red rug on the stairs and the bronze railings and lamp and the harmonium accompanist at low mass for the "ladies and gentlemen from without" evoke the Holy Masses in the Tuileries where the all-beautiful empress, in her miraculous robes, came out and a staff of chamberlains and marshals swelled with pride, while the emperor slept, as if attentive. Only, here, the "faithful" are, on the contrary, poor devils, surprised to find themselves there, under the semi-benevolent watch of very devotional employees wearing silk-waste gloves, damn!

Click, clack! The two carriages of the administration crammed with "convalescents" culled from the four cardinal points of the Public Assistance (familiarly known as the P.A.) are driven in from the street that passes before the gate of honor, pass the

---

[2]*panem... circences*: Latin for "bread" and "circuses".

gate, and stop before the admission office door to un-
load thirty entrants who, after the customary formalities, inscription, summary visit by the doctor, first
reading of regulations by the captain (chief of surveillance personnel), disperse in the direction of the designated rooms, carrying under their arms the articles
of clothing allotted to each convalescent: namely, a
pair of socks and espadrilles, a shirt, a night cap, a
Prussian blue loose outer coat, a woolen skullcap,
same color (we're in the first days of May; the summer costume: a lighter loose outer coat and a straw
hat, from the 15th of this month), a hand towel, and a
table napkin. So, shall we say, every convalescent is
considered to be in possession of a pair of pants? My
goodness, yes.

"Gallery a bit off, room such as it is!"

And the poet enters a room with a floor much
too waxed for his "incomplete ankylosis of the left
knee, consequent to a rheumatic arthritis." Three beds
that the convalescents must make every morning in
accordance with certain principles, as in the army,
and they must also sweep and wax that parquet which
is, alas! so slippery!

The poet's current companions are a guardian
of a public garden, a quiet fellow, and quite a young
man, barely sixteen years old, with blond hair like an
English girl that an already virile grace enhances
however. He notices the difficulty that the poet has
putting on his left espadrille, puts himself kindly at
his disposition. But the bell rings, one goes to dinner,
slow entry into the refectory, good meal, better than
at the hospital, even the dessert, what a joy! exit in indian file under the somewhat terrifying gaze of the refectory supervisor, after recitation in a loud and intel-
ligible voice of the sempiternal regulations.

Promenade in the garden, a pipe or two, then, for the first day, full of fatigue and excitement – oh but relative! to lie down and nap enough until 6 o'-clock, the hour of soup. Soup very tasty, makes one believe he is at Les Halles[3], word of honor!

The second day is spent between the game of bowls, seated in a small wood separated from the large one by palisades, and the rather well-stocked library. There the poet begins his reading of Lamartine's *History of the Restoration*, after the twice-a-day recommended steam bath. Interesting book although, and because, misunderstood and unknown. Bath amusing as can be.

In the evening, ascent to the singing room. The young man just mentioned sings romances with an exquisite voice, intelligibly executed. While going down to his room and for the night, he is greeted above all by the poet to whom he will recount several days later his proud and distressing story. They will need to meet up again several years and a few months later.

The weeks pass in this manner with no great incident – and a departure with several louis in pocket for "freedom" – definitive?

III

Fine, behold the stupidities that begin again! Let's go, fellow Poverty, fellow Bad Luck, fellow No Chance, go back to your natural "hospices."

And it is, for the second time, the literal palace, but how changed, how somber, since the

---

[3]Les Halles: in Paris, where the first Bouillon Duval was opened.

weeks of apprenticeship! The tall windows with long white curtains resemble the casements of a prison for giants or of some house of fools in a dream.

Ready cash, no longer. Some future money, always certain, but less. While waiting, the same July sun after an interval of one year, but oppressive to-day, as if choleric and spreading cholera in its furor; the same room with high ceilings, one might say low-ered like a tempestuous sky that would be menacingly white, the color of white iron heated white, a mourn-ful white, like a virgin convoy; same head doctor: he seems less paternal, with his new followers who don't appear to be at the same level as the others. Service, at first glance, less attentive. Even the patients who appear more hard hearted; during this month, howev-er torrid and which ought to be unhealthy, not one of them has died, but what bad moods, barely lightened by the National Holiday: small extras, an interior dec-oration, at a discount, due to the collective enthusiasm of the patients: paper garlands and the falsely gilded R. F.[4] on the *tricolore* cartons like garlands. Spent twenty days there.

One more blow to the Napoleonic asylum. In autumn. A wet autumn. Last year, it was a beautiful month of spring weather: there were roses of every color along the balustrades overrun at that time by flowers, today by green and black leaves and branch-es. The trees of the quincunx and of the woods turn yellow in numerous places and the wind carries away the leaves. The wind also cries in the corridors on cer-tain days and the currents of air, always bad, start to become "dangerous," as I am made aware by a Parisian with pulmonary disorder, sent here by mis-

---

[4]R. F.: presumably *République Française*, or French Republic.

take, indubitably.

Fresh, and then some, the ends of night, and one sets about to inaugurate the winter system that consists in folding, lengthwise, in two, the rather thin "blanket" that one had been content until now to lay out with exceptional precision and rigor.

The nourishment that, compared to this, otherwise sufficient and sound, if not monotonous, of hospitals in the true sense of the word, was really so good, so varied, now contracts a taste at one and the same time too little (in the strict sense of the word) and too much. No one among the convalescents attributes this change for ill to the imminent departure of the Sisters. Will their replacement re-establish the good order of before, as well as the really paternal (or maternal if you will) discipline, as regards things of the refectory? Because, here also, some laxity, as complement and corollary, one might be tempted to believe, some disregard for the good administration and equanimity above all, as would be needed to improve, reigns too much and does not govern enough.

I'm bored; the library is all read; familiarity with each tree in the little woods bordering a house of fools (men and women) whose cries can be heard, and what cries! towards midday: *A dæmone meridiano libera nos, Domine!*[5] The cows even, milk cows for those afflicted with pulmonary tuberculosis, that pass by in the clearing in miniature, are no longer amusing and lack the appearance of being amusing any more. This is annoying. Evening appears. One dines in accordance with the rules. To go to bed and not to sleep is stupid... And one mounts the stairs to the singing room.

---

[5] *A dæmone meridano libera nos, Domine!:* Latin for "Free us from the devil in our midst, Lord!"

Funny, that.

As some might say the concretion, the synthesis, the quintessence of popular Parisian musical taste, – romance dominates in it. The old reproductions of this genre persist, but the new ones knock the pants off contemporaries with comic aim. It is in this way that *Comme à vingt ans*, *Moine et bandit*, *e tutti quanti* alternating with *Petit Pinson* or *Carmen*, *vous n'avez pas d'âme*, etc., are much more frequently performed and much better appreciated and, in spite of the somewhat draconian rules here, applauded with a strong backup of "canes, crutches and forearm crutches" than are such and such pieces like *Docteur Isambard* or *Joséphine elle est malade*.

There is, however, a remark, made ages ago, that the faubourgians[6], or those thus called, that is to say the naïve skeptic and the spontaneous mocker par excellence, are voluntarily elegiac... in music and that they are more enamored with sentimental and gasping melodrama, pink and black, than with vaudeville and farce. No conclusion otherwise to draw from that, as with three quarters of all remarks, right?

But what performers for the most part! The three historical songs (I'm serious) of the period we have just come out of harmed us all a little, – *En revenant de la Revue*, *les Pioupious d'Auvergne*, *le Père la Victoire*, – pretty as possible like a bell, and like "poems," amusing, spiritual, very spiritual even, even though there are always certain delicate souls who will be unhappy, and feel tormented! False gestures like the guttural and sluggish if not cracked voice, O Paris! or at that time terribly meridional! Unusual pronunciation that makes one wonder whether

---

[6]faubourgians: those who live in the Parisian faubourgs; i.e., the common people.

the singer understands what he "belts out," rhymes terminating in "ô", in imitation of some "artists" of very infamous café-concerts, and this, with chic, with a naïve, fundamentally, and quasi-touching dandyism... ô. And those pleasant topographical saws, if one can say that, where all the quarters and monuments of the capital march past with spiffy tunes, in circumstances that are always amusing and amusingly recounted, *les Statues en goguette, l'Gaulois du point d'Iéna, la Chaussée Clignancourt, la Samaritaine, Derrière l'omnibus,* that are damningly and fuckingly poorly rendered by those fine blokes, ordinarily impertinent and boastful as much as convalescents can be, but as soon as they are "on the boards"[7] – it's a veritable little scene – frightened, awkward, and clumsy. It is only when they spout out something "serious" that they become comical, except on rare occasions! Romance, already quite ridiculous essentially, takes on proportions of parody as far as the eye can see in those honest mouths where previously raucousness and now bronchitis string together the most astonishing notes. There is also the non-intelligence, if not of the things sung, at least of the intentions of the author, good for nothing or not. For example, *les Boeufs* by Pierre Dupont, admirable poem, his masterpiece perhaps, with the *Pins* and *Sapins,* by the true intense poet who will emerge from his semi-oblivion today, – Can you imagine them, as they were in the epoch in question, interpreted with the affected accent of a yokel from Séne-et-Ouése? And the patriotic song! Poor tall cuirassiers of Reischoffen, grievous Alsace-Lorraine, with Marceau's completely beautiful and completely pure face, – at least be clement to

_____
[7]on the boards: on stage.

"your bards" of these parts, with the thought moreover that these are the poor, the infirm, the suffering,
the simple for the most part, sincere in the choice of
their "numbers"; it could well be even that there are
among them some survivors of the epic charge, who
weep, still mightily proud, for the fatherland; that that
kid who bawls "*Il est mort ce soldat stoïque*" has, in
his bag of a *scholar*, the leaf from his collar and the
stars from his sleeve; that that fine boy with the German accent is a deserter from the army of the Reichs-
land...

> But what is that voice? The poet knows it and
does not know it, or the other way around. The false
light, not from the footlights, because there are no
footlights, but from some gas lamps in the room that
their frosted-glass globes discolor obscurely, only
permitting after a while to see the traits of that person
who occupies the stage at this moment, and he dis-
covers that it's the young man from last spring, grown
a bit taller, and that the *leggero* tenor voice has mutat-
ed over the short interval into a velvety, clear, and
warm baritone...

> What else in particular is here before moving
on for good, maybe, and with no more emotion than
is appropriate?

> Ah! if one wishes, this:

> The convalescents' visitors are also allowed to
visit the divers parts of the establishment, under the
escort of an *ad hoc* employee who points out interesting things to them. This honest *cicerone* never fails to
draw the attention of his audience to two immense
maps of Europe and the Two Worlds, the work of a
convalescent, painted in fresco on two walls of the
game room. And he proffers this:

> "That convalescent, on top the time, one year

about, that he was allowed to spend at the asylum in order to bring his work to completion, obtained from the Direction a sum of five hundred francs, and the assurance, or rather the certitude, of an immediate position in a government office. Now, on the day of his release and a few days later, two or three at most, following it, he got drunk, lived it up with the women, in short he spent his five hundred francs and had the audacity to return and solicit assistance which was naturally refused to him."

One has to hear the indignant objections on the part of the good people, relatives, poor for the most part, of the poor pensioners whom they come to see: "Ah!, the bastard! Must the good folk always suffer for the bad? Five hundred francs in two or three days!"

Eh, my fine fellow; eh, my dignified matron; eh, my poor children, have you yourselves often had five hundred francs at your disposal? And do you imagine the turmoil, the literal unhinging in the soul of an artist perhaps, from the lower class, that such a miserable fortune "to gain paradise in a single shot" can do? Does it not appear totally dictated, this conduct, at first sight absurd, with its ancient inveterate despairs, contempt for the future, disgust for the past, indifference for a life that will certainly! recommence more harsh and more distressing...

Days pass. Convalescents, nay "invalids," are seen to the door! There is an end to everything. The poorest will go spend three days in a vague annex where one is charged with helping them find work.

The others spread out through the city in quest of a job that is hiding somewhere and with their health in ruins, like bats in the winter in Paris where the swallows, according to romantic tales, would be little chimney sweeps.

Click, clack! whip, coachman! The two carriages of the administration, packed with "convalescents," moves beyond the metal gate of the courtyard
of honor...

Goodbye, comrades! – or farewell, then!

IV

And behold the diver, deliberation in the
reeds, annihilation, half-stuck, half-drowned, in this
Marne, utter poverty. The only quivering willow
branch, the unique providential board, floating as yet
a little within reach, this will be yet another Hospital,
thanks to the malady that lingers, good but slow pur-
veyor to Death.

And let's go for the third and fourth and nth
time to the building on stilts, exterior slaughterhouse,
intimate Methodist chapel. Change of service. Old
men, this time the *chronics*[8] as they say here. (Chronics, they're practically *saturnine,* really.) Ah, well!
long live old men! They have their problems, primarily physical, but one overlooks them, in virtue of their
morality which, fundamentally, here, being simple
people, finding themselves scant endowed with instruction and reading, charmed by the poet's initial
and intact sagacity and his experience of the *facts*,
facts attested to by their troubles even, as sadly
ridiculous as those troubles might be, sometimes, and
by

"The great poverty

---

[8]*chronics*: chronic alcoholics.

Of the poor wandering Jew"

that you are, a person that one pushes around and that one abuses and who rebels against you, but who is always vanquished, the vanquishment of francs and of privation in exhaustion.

But do they not see that the poet has just practiced the most impossible socialism, and one asks forgiveness for him from the beautiful ladies who will not have read this.

True processions in profound masses, of doctors and pupils. All the doctors with their nuances, kind and then some, for the most part. The pupils, not all. For the majority who are amiable, informed, sufficiently attentive, there are others who are dreadful, abominable, really! poseurs and boors, treating the patient as a veritable prisoner, like a convict, from the top of their wing collars and their light-colored ties with false jewelry, completely inhuman and "insolent," as the so on-edge people of Paris say so well. The poor amongst them, on the *following* day: even in their provincial holes where their "studies" would have led them (them there are the class "dunces"), rancor will not spare them from the miserable wretches who continue to be maltreated and, what's more, at that time, held to ransom, by these rotten doctors. The poet perhaps, also, in the "Invectives" more like Martial than Juvenal, will mention them without praise, those little prigs who will have held him up to ridicule, on his bed of grief and famished. That day then will be terrible, *dies irae* in miniature, and their name, poorly suited for posterity, however, will arrive, in the company of many others, who are surprised. One intern also, *only one*, was vile and spiteful. His name also will ring out when the

time comes. But let's hasten to say it, for the glory after all of this lamentable humanity, that these men are
but a small exception.

One gets used to it in this life of a monastic,
without, alas! the orison, and the rule followed for its
own sake. The bed gets under your skin. One lives
there completely. Even thinks there. Often sluggishly,
sometimes virilely and nobly. The poet does not sleep
there, but outside its the same thing, except when his
bed is shared in certain conditions of good fatigue.
One ratiocinates, one ends up no longer missing the
outside, even ancient, and from that moment on regrettable in the sense of the uninitiated.

And then there were some memorable depar-
tures in those nearly two years of this sort of captivity, less the stability, the prestige! and the seriousness.

Because, on the one side, thanks to unexpected provisional resources (O those resources, O that
unexpectedness, or that provisionality!), a trip to a famous seaside resort was realized. A cure – as if for
some rich person – in the mountains that are the very
respectable foothills of the Alps, and celebrated by
the greatest French poet along with Villon, Ronsard,
and Racine, concurrently with the very blue lake that,
moreover, our very own poet didn't see, for lack of
money for excursions by carriage, but he saw its
mists, half-way up a famous peak, like an eyebrow on
a somber, fantastically gigantic face. Showers and
baths. The buffet supper got smaller day after day (the
saison draws to a close) until the poet remains alone.
Excellent fish, among other particularities of local
cuisine, which are called *pollan*, and several sorts of
really good aboriginal cardoon the name of which escapes me. Good times in sum, a more distracting in-
terlude than one would have supposed. Divers inci-

dents, one of which comical, and due to poverty itself (rare bird, flower of flowers, paradox!) of the "bather." The same poverty provides him with yet other services. (It has the habit of providing him much when well taken.) Returned to the cradle on stilts where, in parenthesis, two months were passed previously beside a dear friend, also ill, and having departed at the same time, to and from whom letters to and from the illustrious seaside resort were exchanged. Ah! those were fine summer months! – just as later, those were, with another dear friend, six sweet weeks in winter. One exits from there, about as affectionate already as one was, mutually, much more affectionate; it is better than a fraternity, than a friendship at college. It's like a fraternity, a friendship at college transplanted onto a previous friendship. And it's exquisite, believe me.

But, off to the other great departure!

An advantageous sale, by what accident? of a manuscript of verse, opened the doors of the Hospital that had always remained half-open by the kindness of the head doctor, to whom a wholehearted thank you, in these lines. Some weeks, indeed two or three months, ran their normal and even pleasurable life course... then the shadow of destitution returns a little in advance of the thing. And it is in this moment that one summer evening, on a wine merchant's terrace where, in company, the poet, dining on credit, saw him approaching, in the humid shadow of a storm that had broken earlier – a long, haggard, timid form, and so long! That form leaned over him almost spectral, when a broken and raucous, and so feeble, voice said:

"How's that, you don't recognize me, the little singer from over there?"

"Huh, what, my friend, is that you? Sit down then. Waiter, a place setting and a dinner!"

Because the poor child evidently hadn't eaten for a long time. And he was leaving, as he recounted, a hospital, and all the night hostels, two days of that, and he was wandering... in such tatters!

As soon as the dinner, what an honor it was done! was finished, the "little singer" confided in his from then on and *forever* friend, that he hadn't a sou to procure himself a domicile with.

"I'm broke too, but my room which I still have is large, and there's enough room for two."

"But I'm ill, tubercular as a result of chills and privations."

"And my acquaintances in the hospitals?"

And two days later, a little bit better in the stomach, his morale a little lifted, a little oh so poorly, alas? reclothed, the child of honest and pure poverty, the orphan with dreadful parents, the flower and fruit of a love two times culpable and criminal to boot! the abandoned fellow, all except by a much older man as poor as he was, but less suffering healthwise, entered the Louis-Philippe establishment of '48, ill and miserable again, *in the barracks*, where the poet didn't delay rejoining him, and those were once again some relatively and positively delicious weeks, even if made melancholic by the young man's slowly worsening condition, who soon, too soon, doubtless, departed again for the Napoleonic asylum, from which he maintained a correspondence with the poet. Suddenly, this latter stopped receiving letters, to his great disquietude. He made some inquiries, learned that the "convalescent" had left the asylum with a *bad cold* (the good A.P. does this sometimes). And no news after this information. Forgetful or dead, the child however so nicely, so touchingly, recognizant *viva voce*?

Be that as it may – and because everything does not always, even in France, have a rosy ending – that doubly painful incertitude came to sadden immensely his final, he hopes this time, escape from hospital stuff.

And without anything more than this for assurance, not to pick up again one day this almost Silvio Pellico-like work, it is in complete melancholy of the past and for the future that he takes his leave of the too benevolent reader whom his pages were able to "distract," and of you, dear Madam,[9] whom they should have, for lack of something better, amused.

---

[9]Madam: most likely Eugénie Krantz, the muse of Verlaine's book of poetry, *Chansons pour elle (Songs for Her)*, which was published in the same year as *My Hospitals*, 1891.

Hospital Chronicles

I

Week and a fortnight when poets will have
made themselves talked about, in diverse fashion, as
is their wont: young poets primed by older ones (by
means of the intermediary, if you like, of a street journal), a real, decorated poet! another ironic and as if
avenged in advance, that one, dead in the hospital,
and... a street in Paris named after the poet who died
in the hospital, by virtue of deliberation by the municipal council of the "City of Light"!

The press has in a dignified manner spoken of
the so original and much missed Maurice Mac-Nab;
on the other hand, all of literature applauded the dis-
tinction that Maurice Bouchor, the author of so many
charming and profound works, found himself the object of, and the Benjamins of Parnassianism distin-
guished by their quite older brothers are quite naturally proud of the mark of satisfaction as well as the au-
riferous windfall. And I will leave them to their joy,
those dignified ephebes, and the competent public to
its legitimate satisfaction in front of the decree that
honors the good bard of *l'Aurore* and *Symbols*, and I
will only focus, in this first Hospital Chronicle, on rue
Hégésippe-Moreau.

"New street," says the official document. And
bravo! A poet's name, above all a man like that one,
smelling good of the grace and youth cut down in

their prime, could not in all decency replace so banal or trivial a sign as one marking a public highway.

And as for an illustrious or traditional denomination, when it was a question of rebaptising it in his favor, it was a good idea not to employ the memory of a charming spirit who would have stoked the suspicion even of a commensurate brutality...

Hégésippe Moreau, a rather effaced figure these days, was a poet, in sum, independent of any school of poetry. Without a doubt, his verses, for the most part, recall very little, by a sort of incoherence, of the influence of the milieu of letters in which he lived. But what's to be done for a young contemporary of so many often contradictory glories? And one can deplore his Romanticism, more the result of Barthélemy and Méry than of great masters, and his too numerous, rather weak, imitations of old Béranger; but *la Voulzie, Un quart d'heure de dévotion, la Fermière, Jean de Paris*, and other poems are still fresh, generous in spirit, and possess an agile and confident language at one and the same time; finally, his *Contes à ma soeur,* with so rare a chastity, still rarer delicateness, if that's possible, – these are the works that will continue to exist and amply suffice to preserve the smiling and sorrowful memory of poor Hégésippe.

Sainte-Beuve loved him and appreciated him, Féliz Pyat was able to discover in his praise of him eloquent accents that induce pardon for that ferocious revolutionary – a great declamatory writer, but how intuitively artistic! – too many heresies, and so many aesthetic mistakes! Baudelaire had several objections, much too severe in my humble opinion, to the respects that were already paid to his name in his time. He reproached him, among other grievances, for fall-

ing into "democ-rocracy" and goes so far as to treat
him seriously as a "hooligan," forgetting that Villon,
who had been the worst of rascals, in spite of it all, remains no less our Father and our Master; forgetting
also that life was not all rosy for that ardent and delicate nature, easily irritated thenceforth. As for his
death in the hospital, let me not deplore it more than
is right. *Experto crede Roberto*: society, under whatever political regime it might be, – read *Stello*! – is
not big on glorifying poets, who, often, if not always,
run counter to its positive laws, at least quite frequently to its most imperious customs, good or bad,
rather bad, I admit. So then,

> *"And why, if I upset*
> *Your most obstinate vow,*
> *Society,*
> *Would you praise me?"*[10]

as also said a *hooligan*, who would be me, it appears.

And, on the other hand, the poet, however
avid for luxury and also well-being, if not more so
than another person, holds his liberty at an even high-
er price than the comfort, the affluence even of the
first person to come along who could be bought by
the least concession to the customs of the crowd. So
that the hospital, at the end of his earthly stay, cannot
frighten him any more than the ambulance the soldier,
or martyrdom the missionary! It is even the logical
end of an illogical career in the eyes of the vulgar, I
would almost add, the proud end, and as needed!

Hégésippe Moreau did nothing but follow in
a tradition that is far from falling out of fashion. Alas!

---

[10]From *Cellulairement,* the collection of poetry Verlaine wrote
while in Mons prison, but which he never published as such.

was I not just reading recently, in a fine chronicle by Jean Lorrain, the tragic details of the recent death of two Slavic poets? And who knows what the future holds for that long list of illustrious wretches since Homer? The word of the Gospel, – to speak so loftily, – is primarily true as to the light-minded race of men that Plato exiled with a crown of roses: "For ye have the poor with you always."

This is why, without any irony, it is proper to felicitate "our aediles," who are not always as well in-spired, on their recent decision. Difficult folk, who are not always delicate, could wish that people in power pass measures ensuring that fewer poets die of hunger than they do today, provided that, long after their decease, their names do not shine in white char-acters on blue plaques at the corner of investment properties. But, to begin with, the means? And then, it is in reality, – posthumous publicity on municipal faience, – all that they can do for us, after having housed us neither more nor less poorly than other, equally interesting, disinherited folk, when all is said and done, and is it not already kind of them for the seekers of renown?

But it's all the same in the end, Hégésippe Moreau would have been quite surprised (and yet who knows?) if this belated apotheosis had been fore-told to him, almost as much, I wager (and yet, am I really sure?) as I would be stupefied if informed that a street, God knows when, should be named after me.

II

Decidedly, all the same, the hospital depress-es, in spite of the beautiful month of June we are enjoying, all verdure moistened with rain, smelling good and shining brightly. Yes, the hospital depresses, in spite of philosophy, insouciance, and pride!

> *"We would enjoy ourselves in the bright sun*
> *And under the green branches of oak trees,"*[11]

we, the poets, as well as the others, the workers our companions in misery and "rooms." And long live pure luxuries, and women, pure or not, and real life, full of life, pure and impure!

While waiting, brothers, artisans, of one and of the other sort, workers without work and poets... with publishers, let's resign ourselves, drink our lightly sweetened tisane or coco, let's accept bravely this one his medicine, that one his rinse, and that other one his jigger! Let's take our prescriptions as directed, submit to the injections, may the injections seem smooth to us and mellow the dejections, and let's suppress all objections, at the risk of the always difficult expulsions, even in this month of flowers and hay-making, of days that grow warmer and clement nights, regardless of whether we've burnt a hole in our pockets and debt and hunger wait for us at home.

Evidently, we will leave sooner or later, more or less healed, more or less joyous, more or less sure of the future, – as long as more or less alive. At that time we will think with melancholy, a melancholy that I have already known in my *"entr'actes,"* a little bit furious, a little mocking, grateful alternately, and rancorous because of our moral sufferings among other things, because of inhuman or good doctors, be-

---

[11]*We... trees*: From "The Workers' Song," 1846, by Pierre Dupont (1821-1870). It was considered the anthem of the French revolution of 1848.

cause of vicious nurses or not, because of such and such supervisor who was cursed when one couldn't mystify her, – not by us, by the others! – because she was too good, etc., etc.

And perhaps one day we will miss those *good ole times* when you, the workers, you rested; when we, the poets, we worked; when you, the artist, you earned your *banyuls*[12] and your toddies by portraits of substitutes and pupils and those "frescoes" in the staff room!

Yes, perhaps one day they will come back to us, melodious from the past, those conversations from bed to bed, from one end of the ward sometimes to the other: "Come on, gentlemen, a bit of silence then! This isn't the Chamber of Deputies. Be quiet, number 27, some kind of repeat offender! It's always the regulars who make the most noise!" – those more than animated and nothing less than dramatic discussions; they will come back to us, those sleeps broken by cries of agony, those vociferations of some alcoholic, those awakenings with these kinds of news items: "Number 15 kicked the bucket. – Did you hear that swine number 4 last night? What a filthy-sounding snore, name of God!" Above all, everything will come back to us, alas! in the shape of useful regret, that sober calm, that strong sense of security found in those places of grief, certainly, but also in the sure medical attention they provided, and bread on the board.

Maybe one day when death taps us on the shoulder, when our incipient and harbinger malady grabs hold of us feverous and painful, maybe poor and alone, we will see them, not without emotion and

---

[12]*banyuls*: wine produced in the Banyuls-des-Mers region of France.

a sort of sadness, – O quite sad! – gratitude, those
long avenues of really white beds, those long white
curtains, because all is long and white, in some sort,
in those asylums.

Everything except, on that supreme day of
June, for me, tired of so much poverty (provisorily,
believe it, because I'm so habituated to it, me, for five
years now!), the Hospital with a capital H, the atrocious idea, evocative of an inexpressible misfortune,
of the modern hospital for the modern poet, who can
only find it, in his hours of discouragement, black like
death and like the grave, like the cross on a tomb, and
like the absence of charity, your modern hospital,
completely civilized as you have made it, men of this
century of silver, mud, and spit!

III

Damn! Will I leave Charybdis then only to
find myself faced with Scylla, and my name, which I
would like to keep purely and good-naturedly poetic,
will it pass into proverb? Already someone, who believed he was doing the right thing, said that if others
had made use of the hospital in order to die, me, I
made use of it (in other words, took advantage of it)
in order to live (in other words, to survive).

However, I give you my word of honor that
my most ardent desire would be to lead the life of so
many others whom I'm the equal of. (And I'm speaking here in complete modesty.) Without luxury, – I
have no luxurious taste, – without too many grand de-
baucheries, – my present health is positively opposed
to them, and my principles (for I do have principles,
don't pretend you don't know about them, O my dear

comrades!) would have some objection to them, without posturing, or excess nastiness, or abuse of kindness, a proper place between the worst and the best; not virtuous, alas! but not vicious properly either; neither Alcestis, nor Philinte,[13] however – finally the life of a good fellow and an *honest man*, in case the latter should need to shoot at a gentleman,[14] because fie on the "gentleman!"

> *Hoc erat in votis.*

Instead of that, for four enormous years (I am keeping track) nearly passed, it is inquietude, what am I saying? it is gasping for breath, it is:

> *Death and desire and money,*
> *Good couriers with diligent feet,*

relentlessly in pursuit of poor me

> *... Always in quest*
> *Of a good meal, of a sure abode,*
> *And who capers like a young goat*
> *Under the crooks[15] of an entire race!*

As a sorrowful poem of mine from several years ago lamented. It's after more than a year of almost insupportable physical and mental sufferings, treasons I keep a lid on today and struggles I will tell, and with

---

[13]Philinte: a character in Molière's *Le Misanthrope.*

[14]shoot at a gentleman: presumably in a duel, which was fashionable at this time.

[15]crooks: in the sense of a Shepherd's crook.

short but yet too long intervals of deceptions, disappointments, appetencies, and disgusts, – the Hospital for four years now (I repeat, I'm keeping track of it), in less than two months.

My character, fundamentally philosophic, my constitution having remained robust despite cruel and above all the most incommodious fits and starts of malady, rheumatisms, bronchitis, stomach problems, and now the heart! have kept me thus far solid yet of body – and of mind! On the other hand, I have only praise for the good attention and assiduous care that until now I've been the grateful object of; excellent friends have done for me what they could, even if other friends have let me down as they pleased and disappointed me with the best faith in the world. I admit all that, and also that I have had in my misfortune what some might call luck. But it is always hard, after a life of work, in short, livened up, I concede, by accidents for which I'm largely at fault, and catastrophes perhaps vaguely premeditated, it is hard, I say at forty-seven years old, in full possession of a good reputation (OF SUCCESS, to speak in the hideous modern fashion) to which my highest ambitions might aspire, hard, hard, very hard, and more than hard, to find myself, my God! yes, ON THE PAVEMENT, and to have merely, in order to rest my head and nourish my body, which grows old, but the pillows and meals of Public Assistance, still uncertain, and which can dry up – may God, moreover, bless it! – for no visible fault on the part of whomsoever, oh! no, not even, and above all not for my fault.

Let someone object with me about Gilbert's sad death, the *key* to which is yet to be found, that of the poor Hégésippe, whom I spoke of earlier, Edgar Poe's appalling end, the lamentable last days of our great Villiers, in order strongly to persuade me that I am a "lucky bastard" to be able to drag out my ripe old age to where I'm hailed, and I dare say, loved by all lettered youth, amidst the drab odor of iodoform and phenol, intellectual promiscuities against nature, the slightly mocking indulgence of doctors and pupils, all the horror finally of a literal poverty poorly protected against the last extremities...

Whatever you might say, or do, it is, – to borrow the phrase of the illustrious Margue, whose STATUE was recently inaugurated!! amidst grand official and *parliamentary pomp...*

It is annoying!

IV

The bed I occupy *this time* at Labrousse Hospital and which has the number 27 *bis* on it, in the Seigle ward, has this particularity that, based on the memory of a patient, no one who has slept there, save two or three original occupants whose numbers I exaggerate perhaps, hasn't died there; this, with a touching regularity of example given and followed.

Such a funereal privilege surrounds this much too hospitable bed with a vaguely respectable consideration, to which a *sui generis* superstition is not completely unknown. In a word or in a hundred words, "it's not an amateur."

As for me, I didn't have a choice. It was a matter of taking it or leaving it. In one sense, leaving it would have almost tempted me; while taking it meant avoiding worse shelters, so I took it.

I took it, not without having seen anymore my predecessor, however, whom I didn't recognize any longer, as they say.

He was still there, my predecessor, when I entered the room. Neither handsome, nor ugly, nor, to tell the truth, anything. A long and narrow shape, wound up in a sheet with a knot under the neck, and no cross on the chest, right on the mattress on the iron bed without curtains surrounding it, just like three quarters of the hospital beds are now. – Still a legend that endures, as my eminent colleagues and my masters in journalism might say. A stretcher named the *box of dominos*, covered by a canopy, dyed some color, a mattress canvas nuance rather, was carried, the package placed on top of it, and off it goes for the amphitheater. Several instants later, I was installed in the just-a-moment-ago mortuary "dusty bed,"[16] and veritably answerable to the slang word I just employed, if one wants to refer to the *pulvis es et in pulverem reverteris*[17] of the Catholic Church.

Besides, it's really extraordinary because one gets familiar here, from the get-go, with that familiar and terrible thing; and, even so, so banally consoling and liberating: death. Eh, what! in ordinary life, – I'm not talking about the death of dear ones, parents or friends, I'm talking about whomsoever, strangers, – huh, what! what an affair!

It's almost frightening; the poor inoffensive cadaver terrifies, or nearly so. When I climbed my numerous floors, if I knew that on such and such a landing, behind such and such a door, at the back of such an apartment, there was... "a dead person," as

---

[16]dusty: the slang word in French is *poussier,* which means coal dust literally, but whose spelling is possibly a corruption of *pucier,* which would be closer to *puce*, which means flea. A dusty (dirty) flea-ridden bed.

[17]Ecclesiastes 3:20: "all are of the dust, and all turn to dust..."

the little girls with their totally pretty, totally round mouth say, I shivered in spite of myself and continued climbing very quickly.

Happy times relatively! Since, even before my present afflictions, my sad – and so silly! – experience saved for me these kinds of, fundamentally, delicious emotion.

But, name of a name of a thousand names of names! I have made progress in skepticism, and, without posing like a vampire or like the least of all country bumpkins in the world, let me boast of a kind little act of seeming sacrilege on the outside, if I can speak thus, in view of better elucidating my thought.

Think on it then! I bury the cobbler of La Fontaine's sham dead man, I dig up his bearskin vendor, I flatten that excellent curate Jean Chouart;[18] I don't even don a dead man's shoes for real, fie then!

No, but – and however that may be, as I avowed earlier besides, in all frankness, a bit unwillingly or by very premeditated immodesty or impudence (which is, fundamentally, less probable), – I lie in his bed, *my* dead man's, I lie, do you hear me, in *his* bed, in his bed which is still... cold!

A bit like the 1830s, my chronicle today. But, what the devil do you want? In this century moving like a *train* at breakneck speed, is it not at all sometimes precious to make the machine go in reverse?

V

Also, is it the fault of the P.-L.-M. (*Prepare the*

---

[18] I bury... Jean Chouart: a reference to the poem by La Fontaine entitled *Le curé et le mort* (*The Curate and the Dead Man*).

Handcuffs!) Company,[19] which makes its omnibus trains traverse all of Burgundy and stop at all the stations? Stations like Vougeot, Beaune, Mâcon, and so many others like them all, by Jove!

And at Mâcon there are two hours of stopover after I don't know how many centuries riding in the wagon, diluted only just by evasions of morally correct behavior:

The moral moment of a glass or two glasses

(as Coppée pretty much said somewhere), from that miserable Paris which seems to withdraw reluctantly, as one moves away from it, oneself, at least momentarily, with some of the naïve and petulant joy of a schoolboy on holidays.

So, a poet (he is still), and that's all there is of late, all the better in the latest fashion, in a word, which makes for a greater success in these articles! Poor like Job, just as proud, a good fellow and violent, and, despite appearances and what people say, not what one calls a bohemian, not by a long shot. His horror of *literary* brasseries is only equaled by his paucity of repugnance for the hospital when he is ill, which happens to him quite a number of times! since forty years old and the years contemplate him. And it is even by one of these contemporary Parnassians that he was, only recently, directed, for his bouts of rheumatism, to visit the miraculous Aix-les-Bains, by the Faculty, jealous to conserve at this "end of the century" so consequent a quill.

---

[19]Prepare the Handcuffs: in French *"Preparez les Menottes!"* *(PLM): i.e.,* The P.L.M. Company, or *Compagnie P.L.M.*, founded in 1857, and which actually stood for the Paris to Lyon to the Mediterranean Railroad Company.

Our man did not miss, assisted by some thirst – it's funny how one has always got a thirst mostly when one is not thirsty – to descend and examine like a good tourist, if not like too prudent a patient, the wines offered along the road – buffets and refreshment rooms – by the relatively conscientious café owners; so much so that at Mâcon (everyone descends at Mâcon!), he felt hot and ran to the Saône, whose rapid course didn't tempt him to take a dip, but on the banks of which he hastened to salute, as was his duty, the statue of Lamartine buffeted by the wind! wearing superb boots and what a beautiful overcoat!

Some reflections on the comfortable garb of poets *in illo tempore* occupied him for several instants, but it started to rain (and with the Saône, what a lot of water, what a lot of water!).

Entering a neighboring café was inevitable. There he drank, by way of aperitif, (fie on the Helvetic Pernod and on the German bitter) a plain bottle of that precious French wine that the noble poet had so loved and, it is said, did a little commerce in, not without profit, and misfortune! behold him once again plunged, after those libations to the illustrious Manes, in such and such relative revery of those blessed times when poets found themselves to be great landowners.

All these cogitations, despite a passable dinner duly washed down, were not without darkening a little the dreamer's mood. His ordinarily open and rather gay expression frowned, frowned by degrees, ended up by entering into complete harmony with the costume he was wearing, some mouse-grey thing with, in places, inelegant details, a missing button, a bit of fraying around the buttonholes, some forced laughter about the stitches. His soft hat seemed to him to conform with his sad thoughts, inclining its floppy brim all around his head, a kind of black aureole around his worried face.

His hat! Even though joyous at times, it also, capricious like a brunette, is sometimes completely round, naïve, that of a child of Auvergne or Savoy; sometimes it is shaped like a split cone, in Tyrolean style, and at an angle, over the ear; at other times it is mischievously terrible, one might think they were looking at the coiffure of some bandito, upside down, one flap down, the other up, the front like a visor, the back covering the neck, then correct and flat with a pretty little crease all around the crown, – his fateful hat that he had gaily nicknamed the hat of the *Infortunatus*, his naughty hat that was decorated a short while ago even by a moiré ribbon, less moiré however than the somber hair of the drop-dead beautiful Rita, flower of Brazil, expanding in the heart of all good poets!

And it was dark like the rainy night that had come pouring down when he arrived in Aix where he had to look for a hotel, upon exiting the dusty vehicle of the calamitous P.-L.-M. (*Pursue the Malefactor!*) Company.

Did he find it, the hotel, and after having gone through those probably innocent adventures?

Does he remember, and who knows?...

Whatever the case, the following day, around noon, we discover him speaking with a respectable *landlady* asking her for a room.

"There are no rooms, Monsieur."

"Ah!"

And the poet, without bothering himself with her anymore than she troubles herself with him,

climbs the stairs in order to assure himself of the fact
or for some other reason?

Does he remember, and who knows?...

When a little while later he comes back down
again by a very nice staircase, my faith! and prepares
himself with his bad leg to quit that inhospitable
doorsill, the lady of the house completely surprised to
see him again says:

"Stop!"

"*Pourquoi*? *Per che*? Wat for?"

(For the poet is polyglot.)

"Where are you coming down from?"

"I have no idea... from above!"

"Sir, enough. I am going to call the police
captain."

"Do."

(For the poet speaks French poorly when he
wants to and when he can, compelled by circumstances like this one. And then perhaps a little in jest
also.)

And sitting down on a bench that he found in
the antechamber:

"May I?"

The hostess did not respond, but she examined
in detail the intruder's toilette. What seemed not to
shock her the least was the allure, the bearing, rather
than the material, or than the *intrinsic*, so to speak, of
that toilette, which was completely novel in her eyes,
which were spoiled by the high-society, chic, and extreme elegance of spa towns.

The hat had certainly its opinionated expression, the irregularities of clothing also, but what surprised her most of all was this, I am afraid: a certain
Cashmere scarf, with a nuance of thirteenth century
stained glass, tied casually around his neck, but with-

out the accepted good grace.

(For the poet is a dandy.)

The police captain arrived finally. Commencement of the habitual interrogatory; but the poet:

"Madam is doubtless habituated to more illustrious guests. I am not the Queen of England, nor the King of Greece, nor even General Boulanger. However you will admit, Monsieur the Police Captain, that I have the right, me who am not the Son of Man either, to rest my head somewhere, on this earth, which is not yet the realm of Heaven."

The captain:

"Have you got papers?"

"Here you go."

"Very good, but Madam suspects you of having gone upstairs, in spite of her having told you that there were no rooms available to..."

"To steal the furniture?"

"Something like that."

"Ah really?"

And, unbuttoning his jacket nimbly, not without however some interior satisfaction and the total aesthetic of having been able for an instant to pass for an equal (an important point) of the great François Villon, the poet continued:

"See for yourself, sir, *Vide, Thomas*, empty my pockets."

"*Sufficit*," said the police captain, a man of wit. "I see you are recommended by Monsieur Doctor ***. Let me take you to him."

And he hailed a covered vehicle; *a landau*, no more no less than as appropriate for a high functionary of the R. F., or some royal guest, or even still some candidate...

The hostess to the poet:

"Monsieur, pardon me, I... My God, I took you for a robber."

"All is forgiven."

But at heart, as he was flattered, because of Villon, to have been taken for a "bad fellow"! He had been quite certain that his appearance, quite unlike Lamartine's, had been taken, recently and long ago, for this and for that and, on other occasions, for an assassin. Only the interrogatory having demonstrated that the guilty had just been guillotined, the affair had THEREFORE no sequel. But to see oneself taken for a robber, that was child's play.

And behold a man, "his heart at ease," and sobered up, because he had been drunk?

Does he remember, and who knows?...

Meanwhile the landau stopped in front of the hotel steps.

The police captain:

"Please get in. And it's the good doctor himself who will be surprised by such an *official* arrival within our walls."

The hostess with a thousand smiles:

"Excuse me again, Monsieur. But you are dressed so amusingly..."

And the poet, tickled pink this time by *his* dandyism, gestured goodbye to the good woman with a wave of his hand so graciously executed that Charles X or Lamartine themselves would have envied it.

"Doctor," the poet said, when the carriage had brought them to the skilled physician's place. "It's me, so and so, on behalf of Doctor X***. And permit me to introduce myself, for the case is glorious if ever there was one, glorious and rare! *Under the aegis of the Law*, Mossieu!"

Please excuse the faults of the author.

VI

I have an enemy.

Here. At the hospital. Yes! Oyez!

Monsieur Leconte de Lisle had already done me and does me still the honor and pleasure of detesting me. Why? Because I was the first to see him again freshly decorated August 15, after the collapse of the Commune, epoch when he let his beard grow and was in the habit of fearing me like the plague because I had remained at my desk at Hotel de Ville at the job I had held for seven years running. Did ever so much bile enter into the soul of devotees of the sacred bull Apis and all the Vedic cows and other ancient curiosities? Whatever the case, he's got it in for me, as they say, based on the information I got that he, before witnesses, who naturally related it to me, for it was less than one year ago, said this about me: "Ah that guy, he's still alive! He will never die then. Unless it be on the scaffold!"

Like an old aunt condemns a prodigal nephew or a womanizer.

One of my former professors of Bonaparte, *recenter* Fontanes, *nunc* Condorcet, a Mr. Perrens, author of things on Jérôme Savonarole, if I'm not mistaken, and who more than once dealt me some nice punishments, passably merited, after all, recently had the occasion to speak about me to many of my friends and jeered at me and at the Decadents, whom he believed I was the "leader" of.

"I was never able to finish *les Soirées de Mé-*

dan,"[20] he added as a kind of proof.

Women also, oh! for the ordinary reasons! perhaps even some probably compromising, although unconscious author of pastiches of the great and dear Mallarmé, bear me feelings that are nothing short of tender. But neither prigs of any category, nor more-or-less interesting Ariadnes, nor little failures of language or rhythm, as entertaining as they might be, will not have amused me, in the divers manifestations of their ill will, like the animal that I ask you the permission to present to you freely.

I would pardon him and not speak about him, if it had to do with one of my dear colleagues in the same precarious situation (isn't it a little, at least one says so, our favorite sin: envy?) or a good but limited worker, a bit rough around the edges and a good talker, or some peasant, even from the great *banlieue* of Paris, or some typical scoundrel, one of those one runs into sometimes in hospitals, half procurer, half *hobo*; but no, neither lard nor pork, my guy, an honest good for everything, a legal good for nothing, qualifying as a day laborer and usurping this title, which implies strength and courage, such that the titular might be a porter at the covered market or a year-round merchant, according to the season, or *et cœtera*, – an acrobat of facile and more-than-superficial professions, an *extra* in the dives called cafés, in the eating establishments upgraded to restaurants *proprio motu*, a controller in the sub-café-concerts of the sub-county towns of Seine-et-Oiseaux, – what's more, also, superintendent at some somewhat suburban or pene-provincial civil interments, adjutant member of non-

---

[20]*Les Soirées de Médan*: a collection of six short stories about the Franco-Prussian War, by various Naturalist writers including Émile Zola, J.-K. Huysmans, Paul Alexis...

existent municipal bands and chapeau-chinois har-
monies so utterly local that they escape the cadastre,
in a word, the idle "mover" and self-important, re-
sounding non-entity...

He is ugly, with an angular face that has the
most deplorable red tint to it, rotten teeth, and his eye,
atrociously blue, sticky, with a beard like a chamber
pot brush that would be moldy, shabby, not without
pretension at having been handsome once (he curls,
or uncurls rather, the *quarantine*[21]), his accent more
that of a country bumpkin than of the faubourg, a
straggler and a stammerer. As well, a *malade un-
imaginaire*, which would be saying too little, a false
sick person, which would be saying too much, an *ex-
pressly seriously* sick person, and that, it seems to me,
is that. Submissive to the cold-milk routine, he has
some of his milk boiled on the sly, – it's easy, before
the reveille, in the office (where there is a fire burning
night and day) – waters down a good hot soup that he
yields almost immediately into a bedpan destined to
be shown to the head doctor at the time of his visit at
9 o'clock, and, with his stomach thoroughly relieved,
he dips slices of bread into milk that is iced according
to regulations. In this way, one secures for oneself
several months in the hospital if a stomach ache and
his cards are played right.

I was no sooner lead by the intern on duty,
whom I had the pleasure of knowing, into the small
room with six beds where that Bit of Love slept (we
have given him, my roommates and I, this sobriquet
by antiphrasis), when he began to mutter almost in-
audibly against that "favor," – ordinarily, it is the reg-
istry office clerk who escorts, then the monitor who

---

[21]*quarantine*: presumably a beard grown in a period of
quarantine.

introduces, new arrivals. My informal manner and my conversation at once familiar with one and all, no sooner left alone with my new "bed fellows," seemed to surprise him a little, rather favorably; then my books and my journals and reviews, unpacked, excited his rather malevolent curiosity. He sniffed at me and kept himself, so to speak, on the defensive, the imbecile who mistook me in the first place for an adventurer! felt me out as to my *profession*, and when I told him that I didn't have one, he didn't appreciate my frankness, which seemed to him injurious and quasi-allusive; but his hostility exploded like a bomb after the first visitors I received. The top hats and the remarks, for him esoteric, by my friends frightened him for good, and as I know a fair number of people who are pleased to enjoy what I write, their tone of voice shows a bit of deference, even though I commonly put my interlocutors as much as possible at their ease, their sympathy at times very expansively expressed made the ears prick up on that ill-conforming head, with what indefinable feeling, envy and curiosity, hateful indiscretion, and all the *et cœtera* of a trivial absurdity!

He tried at first to harm me by digs from behind my back, repeated to me, meanwhile, faithfully by the generally good fellows of my hospital entourage, indeed by words stinking of malevolence spoken in the vicinity of the personnel; then, taking off the mask after several attempts at conversation with me, touching on individuals that he happened – by what chance? – to really know, then touching on things related to those people that it was forbidden for him to think about, which it was soon impossible for me not to make him be aware of, he gave himself over to indirect and then direct teasing, like opening or closing doors in my face in order to annoy me, words of double meaning about the "misunderstood poets" and the "bohemians" and the *protégés*, oh! above all the protégés, less indisposed than desirous of eating the bread of poor peeps after having gotten fat off their sweat. All of it until I got angry and responded to him as he deserved and sometimes better.

Then that transformed into the bitter-sweet plaintive and bad behavior on an order completely deceitful. As the individual's character inconvenienced the other patients as well, and as they, like me, no longer responded to his atrabilious or moaning humors, it didn't take long before he left us alone somewhat; but his rancor (towards what, my God?) took a new turn, which was to peddle a little bit everywhere that I was an abominable cleric, a "Bonapartist" unworthy to sponge off a too kind R. F., veritably! – because I had, on several occasions, gently defended the good God in favor of this cretin, and even, O crime! manifested several vague Boulangist impulses, however so discreet they might have been...

Finally, the trick, belatedly discovered, of the prolonged bedpan was brought to the dear attention of that perfect example of a *batter*, or, if you prefer, hospital *pestal*. The two vocables are of a most pure and special slang, and I highly recommend them to our documentary novelists.

The moral of all this is that Envy, in the Latin sense as in the other, will squeeze its way into everything and that its place is not only, as the intensity of the expression would seem to indicate, at the pulpit of great schools, in the armchair of the academician, or on the sofa of the bourgeois and the tart, any more than on the imitation leather seat of "intellectual" brasseries, – and that it is consoling for humanity,

which is not much more thoughtful than such a door-
man, that that collector of *lost objects* and *sequins*,
that the fine, premier merchant of countermarks and
tutti quanti, cedes no ground, in terms of bile and
vinegar... to Mr. Leconte de Lisle, for example.

VII

And to say that this is, since November '86, the third
Fourteenth of July that I will spend in the hospital!
Without being of too irreproachable a Republican or-
thodoxy, I confess that "I adore enough," as Banville
says, that celebration and its rites: amusing dances,
rather decent, as they take place in the middle of the
public square as in the village, especially at dawn or
at dusk, to the sound of street organs replacing the ex-
hausted and gone-to-bed orchestras; the marching
past of kids, always nice, amusing little aperitif to the
grand Longchamps parade, already traditional and
legendary, which I joyfully certify is "followed" more
and more by a fundamentally military population,
more patriotic than one thinks outside the country and
among us country bumpkins.
        And then, – the celebrated anniversary, a little
absurd all the same, is not about to displease me en-
tirely. On this day, the people committed their first
blunder by destroying a prison *for nobles*, – but also
their first act of faith, made more sacred, more cordial
still by the naïve spirit of unparalleled disinterested-
ness that it contained. One will certainly plead the relative heroism of those conquerors of some *invalos*
and their contestable magnanimity after capitulation.
No matter! the greater royal privilege, the only truly
odious thing perhaps, was overturned, the *lettre de*

cachet thrown into the basket by the single act of de-
struction of that fortress of medieval or much rather
Renaissance good pleasure – for let's remember,
among other school memories, that it was Francis I
who "unbridled" royalty, the Revolution finally having been inaugurated much less thanks to a brutal
episode, fundamentally banal, than to the help of
symbolism (that's really the word for it), the unconscious symbolism of a throng of people sublimated by
conjectures.

But our contemporaries, who are, I'm afraid,
much less symbolist than decadent – to borrow, in our
quarrel over words, while there is still time maybe,
their very ephemeral vocabulary, – I fear that they
make a mockery, naturally, of these considerations;
and they are right!

And, kids! bring out the artillery? When was it
exactly, near the July Column, in that court of Sain-
t-Francis, when all or almost all the kids on the street,
rich with the *sous* I lavished on them, set the sidewalk
and the roadbed afire with firecrackers and rockets,
and the sky with Roman candles, and the walls with
suns, setting off from between the paving stones,
from above the window ledges, from the ground floor
and from a little bit everywhere, the mischievous
Swiss cones, while mixing in the shrill *Vive Mossieu
Paul!* with *Vive la République!* obligatorily.

And, kids! bring out the rounds and the "bal-
loons"[22] and the "cheeses,"[23] and the *A hen on a wall,
On the bridge du Gard is thrown a ball, It's the*

---

[22]balloons: Parisian slang for a theater dancer's set of puffy
gauze skirts.

[23]cheeses: a game girls play where they spin round while
bending down so that their dress fills out and has a round shape
like a wheel of cheese.

knights on the lookout!...

And everyone! two steps forward!

The good policemen smoke their pipe under their indulgent nose, that day, the deputy sergeants themselves savoring one- and two-cent cheap cigars. The good drunks festoon and hum, in spite of the "bitches" not enraged by that annual exception. A sincere attitude of fraternity that is a tad bit cocky, very songful, for example, floats, one might say, in the folds of the flags and seems to descend from there into the soul of the passersby. It's superb and almost touching, and the R. F., beneficiary that day, with the bridle placed around the neck of the good *populo*, straightens up, fights back, as one says to the regiment, feels twenty-years young, as old as that same puberty made it feel yesterday, and can believe itself as popular for a little while as the late "Badingue"[24] did long ago, and as that "Boulange"[25] did, of recent memory, who was so damned spineless besides.

But, of us others, imprisoned by Misery and Booboos, that R. F., all proud, all joyous, does it think a little at least of us, its poor? Humph, humph! "*Mon guieu voui!*"[26] under the influence of a double ration of wine; altogether a half liter for "the well-behaved patients," and a two- or three-sous gâteau, an éclair, a baba, a small tart; then, in the evening, retirement (not a torchlight procession) at 9 o'clock instead of 8, and permission to sing if we wish. And then there are the *Noëls* (alas! of Adam), the *Rameaux* (of Faure, *holà*), because the Parisian, the man of the

---

[24]Badingue: sobriquet for Napoleon III.

[25]Boulange: General Boulanger.

[26]*Mon guieu voui*: Tourrainian slang for "My Gosh yes!"

faubourg, is not so skeptical that he does not swallow,
until exclusively for real, the "church tunes," and the
Petits pinsons, the *Carmen, vous n'avez pas d'âme*;
for, also, the men of the faubourg and the vagabond
fall for the elegy but seldom fall into the trap of politics (good for the several seventy-year-old long
beards) or for a trick, which would seem attributed to
the couches, a little too comfortable if not much more
intellectual, of bourgeois men in the bud, the student
and the artist in bloom, schoolboys and apprentices or
errand boys, or the little bohemian.

The enthusiasm, and that's totally natural, is
rather subdued, it must be confessed as well. However, it bursts out, in certain zones, in tricolor paper garlands ingeniously twisted, in blue, white, red es-
cutcheons with the obligatory initials in golden yellow; in all, the fruit of a subscription as cheap as one
sou. This, in the north of Paris (I say only what I've
seen, in the seriously democratic North, Belleville,
Ménilmontant). In the South, faubourg Saint-Jacques,
Montrouge, flat calm, nothing.

But, in one of "my" hospitals in those regions,
the patients, so cold (in appearance), I hope that is because their profound feelings are guarded and discreet, as regards the form of our present government,
open up in respectful and grateful manifestations towards their head of service, the illustrious and vener-
ated Dr. ***, at the time of the celebration, which
falls on the feast day of Saint-G***, if memory serves
me. Festoons, astragals, bouquets, compliments. And
the prince of science does not run aground and re-
gales his humble clients in a princely manner with a
beautiful concert, with glasses, prudently but gently
flavored, of tea or of coffee, with gâteaux and sweets,
that for some time infuse joy and gaiety into those

poor hearts who are all gratitude for the fine concern and delicate attention they've received.

But I prefer, however well-known my revolutionary chauvinism might be, that celebration of true Fraternity to thine of yesterday, Liberty, dear Liberty!

VIII

Because this is the last of the series, perhaps definitively the last, and I thought even that it would not exist, this chronicle that I needed to write however in view of filling out an entire little program of impressions that are nowise socialist, as is the fashion nowadays, nor above all *anarchistic*, a stupid word poorly borrowed from the "great" Proudhon of yesteryear by young, likeable, but insufficient people.

So, last December, I was seized suddenly by an atrocious rheumatic pain, that was earlier felt, long before, in the left knee; – this time, it was in the wrist on the same latitude. That happened in the faubourg Saint ***, where exists a vast hospital whose excellent director I had known for a long time, who had me admitted urgently under the care of Dr. T***. This latter was literally so kind, as well as his intern, to me that I felt a literal grief when I was discharged and had to take leave of those gentlemen.

I inhabited a small, windowed room joined to a larger one, in a T shape, such that by the disposition of our beds in a line (we were five of us, of which me the fifth, in a corner) I was induced to compare ourselves to "cadavers in the Morgue"; but the good doctor – familiar with my name – had nicknamed it the "Decadents' room."

The question is whether I was perfectly happy

in this as yet, I hope, last hospital, – no. Only, I lived a tranquil month there, completely in the charming and delicate care of a perfect medical team and the most devoted possible subaltern personnel.

Even my "comrades" were pleasant for the most part and cordial. One among them in particular, a soldier, – what a terrible man, all mustaches! – had just returned from battles in Africa. He had no faith, the good chap, in either God, or the devil (Parisian, to boot); and as I objected to him from time to time that there had to be someone above more clever than we are, and that he was wrong not to believe on, nor to trust in, Him, my Biribiste baptized me "ratichon," which means "curate" in slang. That's all he called me, nothing else, and this sobriquet greatly pleased those among us who had the strength to be amused.

But now I say goodbye to my hospitals of these latter years! If not *au revoir*; then, *salut*! in any case; I lived calm and laborious amongst you. I quit you, one after the other, only to, in some sort, miss you again; and if my dignity as a man was relatively less, not much less, miserable than the most sadly deprived of your regulars, and my just instinct of a good citizen not wishing to usurp the beds, alas! so desired by so many poor fellows, [they] often precipitated me, and ofttimes prematurely, out of your doors so blessed on arrival, but not more than on exit, rest assured, good hospitals, that in spite of all the necessary monotony, all the necessarily strict regime, and all the inherent inconveniences, eventually, in every human situation, I retain a unique memory of you, among so many other remembrances, infinitely worse, that exterior life has done to me, does to me, and will do to me, without a doubt, ever and always.

My Prisons

I

Rue Chaptal. Almost at the corner of rue Blanche, on the right when coming from Notre-Dame de Lorette. A monumental metal gate opening onto a paved courtyard, leading to the refectory of the boarding house L***. On the right-hand side, a small door giving access to the interior of the establishment, on either side of which, hanging, two black panels bearing, in gold letters, a list of the diverse sciences and arts taught at the establishment. An immense wall with interminably long messages, written in heavy official characters half-effaced by intemperate weather, forbidding the application of bills or the deposit of rubbish, in virtue of such and such laws already very ancient, and, behind this, surpassing it by nearly one meter and a half, the low buildings of study halls and dormitories.

All that disappeared five or six years ago to make way for, of course, *beautiful* investment properties with thirty-six floors above the entresol.

It was there that a very long time ago I began my "studies" after having learned to read and write – and count (poorly) in a small elementary class...

I was seventh in my class at Bonaparte secondary school where the boarding house had us conducted two times a week; but as I had fallen behind in my studies, due to some catarrh I had contracted, tutoring was provided, and it was the boarding school teacher, Father L***, who inculcated into us, – for there was a group of us, some of whom were dunces, myself not yet one of them – the principles of Latin, not without an extreme patience sometimes, all the same, in the absence of which, witness whereof what follows.

Rosa, the rose, held but few mysteries for me anymore. *Puer bonus, mater bona..., pensum bonum*, as well. I had crossed, not without difficulties, that dangerous pass of *qui, quae, quod*, and, while waiting for the already suspected torments of that "elided *que!*" no less than the stumbling blocks of a fortunately-as-yet distant syntax, I had reached the second conjugation of active verbs.

It was to *legere* that he turned his attention one certain day.

I still remember the theater of those rather tedious mornings in general for the young boys just separated from their papa and mamma. A classroom furnished with a vast desk, an armchair, mahogany back, leather seat, and a bench and a table with holes drilled into it for the lead inkwells used by the "pupils" that we were. From time to time the lesson was interrupted by the entrance of a drummer-courier of the National Guard, wearing a black *bonnet de police* with checkered borders and a red-and-white tassel, delivering some report at the bottom of which our master, adjutant-major captain, put his signature, and, disappearing with the military salute to which Father L*** responded by lifting his skullcap with its leaf pattern in blue silk thread.

That day then:

"Verlaine, conjugate *legere*."

"*Lego,* I read; *legis*, you read, etc."

"Good. Imperfect?"

"*Legebam*, I was reading, etc."

"Perfect. Preterite?"

Me fresh out of the the first conjugation:

"*Legavi.*"

"*Legavi?*"

"*Lexi,*" whispered one of my classmates to me, "stronger" than me in Latin, with the best intentions in the world.

Me, sure of my fact:

"*Lexi, m'sieu.*"

"*Legavi! Lexi!*" the master howled literally, standing up on his heeled shoes, purple in the face, almost foaming at the mouth, while his marine-blue dressing gown with its red-padded lining floated about his rather skinny legs suffering from some rheumatism, and while a ring of keys thrown vigorously against the wall, to the left of my head, which I had taken in both hands to reinforce it on my shoulders, soon followed by a Noël and Quicherat[27] dictionary, practically a Bottin[28], which came crashing to the right of my head, against the wall in question. A double gaffe, on the part of the teacher, doubtless intentional after all.

And after several trembling steps of forceful rage, perhaps sincere, he said:

"To detention, monsieur!"

A bell was rung and the *valet* (read "errand boy", who did a little of everything: we called him *Lick-wick* familiarly, because of the lamps he lit for our studies in the evening) appeared.

"Conduct this idler to detention."

And behold me in "detention," equipped with

---

[27]A Quicherat dictionary was a Latin-French dictionary. The Noël dictionary had presumably merged with Quicherat by this time.

[28]Bottin: presumably after the name of an author of thick books or directories.

legere to be copied ten times with the French opposite it. A detention room that moreover could be exited, was full of light, without rats or mice, without bolts (a turn of the key sufficed), something to sit on, and, – most unfortunate – something to write with, and which I exited at the end of two hours, probably as knowledgeable as when I went into it, but assuredly with an appetite, soon satisfied, for the love of freedom (the good kind, which is independence) and who knows? with that spirit, likely, of adventure which, when too unbridled, will have me thrown into harm's way, a little bit of every sort of it!

What impressions were mine in that miniature captivity? Naturally, I would not be able to describe them precisely at this moment in my ripe age, already! after so many years and so many slightly more serious bolts closed tightly on my human freedom, for one reason or another, the number of which must include precisely the misuse of conjugation mentioned above, and the humble anecdote that I just related – would it not by chance be a symbol? Did it not constitute, at that time, something like the announcement and the presentiment of misfortunes due to READING? Did it not already stamp upon my childhood the fateful phrase of that detestable, if savorous, Vallès'[29]: "Victim of the Book," which, in good Latin this time, *Legi*?

II
"Now this was happening..."

---

[29]Vallès: Jules Vallès, founder of *Le cri du peuple* (The Cry of the People), a quotidian journal started in 1871 just days before the Commune started.

In 1870, in the month of December. I was a national guard of the 160th battalion, the sector I don't remember anymore, near Montrouge and Vanves. What's more, I fulfilled for a long time already the responsibilities of copyist for the Prefecture of the Seine, employment that would have exempted me of all "military" service were it not for my patriotism (a bit *patrolotic*[30], just between you and me, a matter of conscience, in those times of obsidional fever, suffered by many Parisians, besides). Some love of the uniform – what a uniform! – and a little curiosity, also, encouraged me. In brief, the Ramparts and the Bureau alternated more or less agreeably in my rather comfortable life at that period of time (*Quantum mutata!*[31]). A day at the bureau implied for me a night of young married life; a tour on the ramparts involved a rough sleep, – excellent motive for not getting inured to the works of Mars. Also, after the first shot was fired, my having well savored the joy of wearing the fancy kepi and handling the Tabatière rifle, the Bureau, much reviled in the peaceful days under the "infamous" Second Empire, the Bureau appeared to me, despite the holy Republic, finally obtained after coveted for so long, and despite the danger incurred by a fatherland for which my willingness as a "*pantouflard*"[32] could only really be too little, the Bureau ended up gaining the upper hand over my inclinations for the Ramparts, its tournaments of *jeu de bouchon*[33] in the snow, its cold feet, and boredom! And I neglected

---

[30]patrolotic: a pun on the words patriotic and patrol, which works surprisingly well in English for the French hapax: *patrouillotte*.

[31]*Quantum mutata!*: Latin for "how things have changed!"

[32]*pantouflard*: a Parisian man of a certain age participating in the urban police guard and not going into battle.

my service and its inconveniences a little bit, in favor
of my employment and its compensations, conduct
that soon earned me a visit by the corporal, a good little cobbler from rue Cardinal-Lemoine; the excellent
lad brought an order to me that I should betake myself
to the sector's prison for two days and two nights. I
received the corporal very cordially but the order bad-
ly, and refused to follow the first. The following day,
he rang again at my place, conveyor again of that
same thing, a second time.

Resistance was no longer acceptable, and duly
wrapped warmly in a balaclava, mittens, "covered" in
shoulder straps, with a full tin, provisioned as well
with a terrine of partridge paté (!) by my wife (*quantum*, that, also, *mutata*!), I set out, flanked by my superior, in direction of the post, today demolished in
order to make way for school buildings on avenue
d'Orléans, right next to the Bréa chapel, still standing
and serving as auxiliary parish to the quarter, – place
of detention that has become odiously infamous since
then as a result of the massacre of Serizier, in May
1871, of the Dominican Friars d'Arcueil.

We arrived about two hours after my rather
early morning departure from home because we had
stopped to visit with some battalion comrades acting a
little like wine merchants, and between that and other
stops, at the warehouse, nearby, of Wines, where other comrades, employed there, regaled us "at the
Princess's expense" while wishing me good luck in
my "captivity."

There was a Clerk of the Courts Office where
several sub-officers of the citizen army proceeded
with my incarceration, and a sort of immense ware-

---

[33]*jeu de bouchon*: a tossing game, where a coin is placed on top
of a cork, and two pucks are thrown at it.

house that would have been a grange, which would have been the atelier of a tribe of wholesale painters or sculptors, getting light from above by an immoderately sized, poorly-sealed, glass ceiling, summarily furnished with camp cots all around a stove fed from the outside and with a "cabinet" in a corner, where the traditional Thomas[34] slept, useful and smelling bad.

I entered this gigantic hall of police where a group of thirty, at minimum, prisoners, kepis and pea jackets, talked and sang, smoked and played, dominos, checkers, and chess – or cards! in a word, led a lifestyle that was not bad in the least... for them... The stove raged, the glass ceiling did too, and it was a suffocating heat amidst the cold North winds, exceptionally efficacious vehicles of future bronchitis and rheumatisms on the horizon, and I caught my just retributive allotment from it in due course. Familiarity between my companions and me was effected quickly, thanks to a relatively all around, especially communicative, temperament that I have. The large majority, let's say the totality of my companions, was made up of workers thrown there for minor faults against the discipline, of a sort similar to my own (in all the national guard, it's well understood, discipline, you know,... and then, it needs to be said... looking back: "In war things are different."). The most "over the top" among those fellows was named Chincholle, just like the illustrious reporter, already known at that time, and even that name struck me, – as proof! He was a commercial painter, a good talker, a virtuoso of romantic tales and saws, the resident life of the party.

---

[34]Thomas: a toilet, named after Thomas Crapper, an English plumber who founded Thomas Crapper & Co., a sanitation equipment company. In American-English, we say "the John."

His sentence, one month, attributable precisely to that turn of wit, and some intemperate language vis-à-vis some observation that those outbursts had brought on him, which didn't seem to affect him all that much. O the amusing fellow, full, as well, of common sense, and who got carried away to the letter in "torrential outbursts," manifesting little enthusiasm for "The Thing" in power. And what a resourceful person! From without, by the complicity he'd acquired, thanks to his ruses and his loquacity (his *bragging* in Parisian parlance), each successive guard felt at home with us, across the space taken up by the passage of the furnace pipe to its origin, the deliveries of drops and aperitifs of all kinds, actively expedited, you'd have to see it to believe it. Evening come, each one of us, wrapped in his blanket, stretched out on his bed, and the stories, clickety-clack! tales where women and clergy played the preponderant roles, parading before us in long recitations often amusing, late into the night. From time to time, a shell come from Châtillon[35] or elsewhere whistled over the glass ceiling, barked, whinnied, and went on to surprise into the distance, "into the crowd." I should confess here to my shame that I profited from the shade and repose of two nights behind bars and on that cot, eating, what am I saying? appreciating, savoring the divine partridge paté, in secret, on the sly. Come on, anyone else in my place!...

One spoke politics at times, and it's something that struck me all the more contradictory at that period of my existence given, apparently at least, that I was of a revolutionary nuance of the most engrained

[35]Châtillon: a community outside Paris, where several skirmishes were fought during the Prussian siege of Paris, during the Franco-Prussian war of 1870-71.

sort, Hebertist[36], Babeufist[37], what do I know? – compared to the extreme moderation, mildly skeptical and
comical as well, of all those worthy workers there, the
majority of whom, I'm afraid, remained another five
months in order to expiate the sunburn of the Commune, exasperating their initial common sense in an
insurrection that was merely, after all, in principle.

In these conditions, acceptable all said and
done, my forty-eight hours passed quickly, and it was
easily, but with a great deal of warmth, that I separated from citizen Chincholle, a kind of Constable of the
Maréchausée[38] (remember Dickens and *Little Dorrit*)
and his subordinates of some sort, who escorted me to
the door, as was the custom, with a vigorous and re-
sounding:

> *You're going and you leave us.*
> *You leave us and you're going!*

On return to my Penates[39], I was welcomed, naturally,
kindly, without anyone forgetting to ask how I had
found the partridge paté. To which, on my having responded, "Delicious! how kind of you to have...", it
was replied to me: "I had always, in fact, heard that
rat was one of the finest meats."

---

[36]Hebertist: Jacques René Hébert, a journalist, founder, and
editor of *Le Père Duchesne*, a radical journal.

[37]Babeufist: François-Noël Babeuf, known as Gracchus Babeuf, a
political agitator and journalist at the time of the French
Revolution.

[38]Maréchausée: a military police force that preceded the
establishment of the gendarmerie.

[39]Penates: household gods, or hearth. Scil., home.

III
A... Failed Attempt

The late Arthur Rimbaud and I, taken by a violent case of wanderlust, took off one beautiful day, if I'm not mistaken, of July 187*, for A***, which I had visited and needed to visit on numerous occasions for family business, and the like. Curious town, Spanish-style houses of the good XVIIth century and some monuments, of which the most beautiful French gothic Hotel de Ville, barracks and convent, bells and drums. No commerce and little industry. Some rich families confined behind the white-painted, high--shuttered windows of their little houses with fine gardens. The population, well-off or poor, stay-at-home, but of good composition.

We boarded the train around ten o'clock in the evening and arrived at day. A tour of the town was done quickly, these fortified towns are restricted in size, and while waiting for the persons likely to receive us amicably, without bothering them too much, we resolved to go eat at the buffet in the train station where we drank first one or more aperitifs each... while talking about this and that. Rimbaud, in spite of his extraordinarily serious precociousness which bordered sometimes on sullenness crossed with rather macabre whimsies or very particular fantasies and, me, still a boy despite my twenty-six years of age, we were that day of a mind turned lugubriously comical, and, in a playful mood, we got it into our heads to try and "flabbergast" some of the "friendly" travelers there consuming their bouillons, stuffed bread, and galantines washed down with too expensive Algerian wine! One of the types present happened to be sitting to our right, I still remember it, on our bench, at a small distance, a good man getting on in years, mediocrely dressed, a faded straw hat over a shaven face that was begging to be slapped, simple-minded and sly, sucking on a one-*sou* cigar and inhaling a ten-*centime* mug of beer, coughing and speaking in a hoarse voice, who listened up to our conversation with an attention less stupefied than malevolent. I pointed him out to Rimbaud who began to laugh, as he often did, silently, without making a sound. O the horrified apparition, who vanished suddenly (as if by magic, in *house slippers,* and assisted by our distraction, to tell it straight and not descend into the fantastic as is fashionable nowadays). We had been talking about a murder, robbery, as if *by first-hand knowledge* and in truculent details, one would have said even more than ocular, and we were continuing on with this same theme that we had embarked on, as it happens, – when before us appeared as it were, as if pushed there *subito*, two gendarmes with the most matter-of-fact attitudes, these ones, who invited us summarily to follow them.

We followed, as obliged, the representatives, otherwise respected, of an authority whom we found nonetheless in quite a bit of a hurry to deal with us, *so nowise* reprehensible. Finally! and we crossed, after a good or rather bad quarter of an hour of marching in the narrow streets of market gardeners selling their produce, the three or four steps at the entrance to the lateral side of the town hall, where, I don't know why or how, the fully-competent chief public prosecutor presided, in chambers preceded by an antechamber where we had to wait for him for a while. Pretty good, that side entrance. Arched vault, grey stone and black wood with assorted hangings. The national guards (it was so soon after the war and before the suppression of that militia there) stood guard, dressed nearly, but more opulently than did, like *paquets-de-couenne*[40] during the siege of Paris; these "city agents," they are everywhere the same, with many of the same details nearly, ambled about indolently, as if at home, in fact... Rimbaud, after having made a sign to me, launched into a fit of crying, which was supposed to soften and softened our good fellows of the gendarmes (they are not all as friendly anymore than very sensible at times, even in their irresponsibility) while expecting a response from M. the Public Prosecutor. It was Rimbaud whom they called first, and he exited soon from the important chambers his eyes still moist and with a wink to me by way of warning. I penetrated, in turn, the chambers of the first *standing*[41] prosecutor, who, seated on a circular leather chair that he seemed screwed down on rather, interrogated me, interrupting that formality by not a few rogue observations on the condition of my white pants, somewhat sullied, in fact, by the dust of travel, not to mention some prior and subsequent wear and tear. Several objurgations then muttered: "An execution has just taken place in A***. Regrettable, these topical (*sic*) conversations in a public place and in said circumstances... Can give rise to suspicions *perhaps* correct... The proof... You see... After all, what did you come here to do? With this young man who seems well disposed and respectful of the law? But once again, what did you come here to do? Clad in this way the both of you, and without luggage, right?... Yes... you see what I mean."

I explained my case, whimsy, a walk in the

---

[40]*paquets-de-couenne*: slang for National guardsmen.

[41]standing: State.

country with a friend, – this, clearly, bluntly enough even. I was more Republican than at present, I left being a bit more Communard, and I spoke passably presumptuously. After having given references of locals, presented "papers", letters, passports, legal tender (O Time, suspend your flight!), I added that I was a native of Metz, that I had to choose between France and Germany, and that, my faith! now, I was hesitating, really! in view of this ar-bi-tra-ry arrest, etc., etc. (M. the Prosecutor, – now M. the President, could bear witness to the veracity of this entire account.)

After a little stormy silence, the sound of a stamp by the magistrate, mutton chops on his face, young as yet, with brown curly hair and precocious glasses, was a signal to the gendarmes to enter, to whom it was said: "You are to conduct these individuals back to the train station, where they are to leave by the first train for Paris." I objected that we had not eaten lunch. "You will lead them to get food, but they leave immediately afterwards, and do not let them out of your sight until the train starts moving."

No sooner said than done. A bit concerned about presenting ourselves again at the buffet between our official acolytes, no less also about retraversing the encumbered streets at this hour on an empty stomach, we had a bite to eat at a "good place" that the sergeant pointed out to us, took coffee, then a drop, which we invited the gendarmes to partake of, and, not without trouble because of our pants which our escorts must have given a "sinister" look to in view of the more numerous passersby we encountered, we arrived at our destination. After cordial farewells to these, when all was said and done, kind constables, we piled into a second-class train, full of admiration for the manner, the procedure, even more so for the good judgment, of M. the Prosecutor P***.

And it was with renewed courage that in Paris, that same evening, weighed down by a serious, if not a little better meal this time we took off again, from another train station, for more serious adventures.

IV

The Amigo

Short, but sweet.

Moreover, a pure prelude.

Here we are. In July 1873, in Brussels, where owing to a dispute in the street, consecutive to two shots from a revolver the first of which had wounded not seriously one of the interlocutors and which these two friends paid no attention to, in virtue of an apology requested and accorded at the moment of the act, – he who had committed the so regrettable gesture, besides having been, by bad luck, under the influence of absinthe both before and after, had so energetic a word to say and searched the right pocket of his jacket where the firearm was, still loaded with four bullets and with the safety catch in release – this in such a significative fashion – that the other, taken with fear, ran off at full speed down the vast causeway (de Hall, if my memory serves me), pursued by the furious man, to the astonishment of good Belgians[42] lazing about on an afternoon under a raging sun.

A town policeman who was strolling through the area didn't delay seizing delinquent and witness. After a very summary interrogation in the course of which the aggressor was denounced by more than the

_____
[42]good Belgians: in the original it's "pons Pelches" which one imagines to be Walloon patois for "bons Belges."

other accused him, and both of them, by injunction of this representative of the army, betook themselves in his company to city hall, the agent holding me by the arm, for there was only time to say that it was me, the author of the murder attempt and of the subsequent offense, the object of whom happened to be none other than Arthur Rimbaud, that strange and great poet who passed away so unfortunately last November 23.

Very well, Brussels city hall in all its gothic style, a little too dreadfully Renaissance. While I didn't see him again, shame! after that adventure, I render him this impartial homage that I was hardly thinking about, as you can imagine, when being led under its porch or rather one of its porches, to the office of the police commissioner, one of the most strict, staid, and stiff, as they commonly are five-sixths of those functionaries or those like them, a little moreover for form's sake in ordinary cases, while in this case it was serious, *for reals*.

After the shortest time, but, thanks to a disregard for me more perhaps than for my companion, with consequences that could ensue for your servant, and the most circumstantial of *minutes* (is that really the expression?), the magistrate released Rimbaud, completely naturally, but informing him that he must remain available for further questioning and decided that I would be conducted immediately to "l'Amigo."

This cordial name, vestige of the Spanish occupation of Belgium during the XVIth and XVIIth centuries, renders well our French word "slammer" in designation of a police station. This Amigo not standing but several steps away from city hall, I was there in no time, escorted by two henchmen, one of whom this time was a police sergeant or sub-sergeant, those stripes being indifferent to me at that epoch and, what can I say? – since then. Not lovely, for example, the Amigo. Clean at best, and proud credit to the country of excessive cleanliness! As I had money on me – that's all, and my clothes, which were left at the police station – they had placed me *automatically* in preferential quarters, which was fundamentally a good thing. But those preferential quarters, getting air and light by a fanlight situated too high up, with, inside it, two beds, two tables, two chairs, and all other commodities, except one, omitted, did not procure for me the concomitant peace: a well-dressed drunk, worst of scourges! after no time at all come to share my fate, made the night in any case insupportable to me. And from outside, singing, cries, yelling, came until the wee hours of the morning. Tunes principally like *La Fille de la Mère Angot*, at that time all the Belgian... rage, assaulted my ears until dawn. A liter of lambic, some cheese and bread, with the hope that they would give me or rather sell me, what's more, a prompt release, made the time however appear quite long. Towards seven in the morning, my door opened, – what bolts! – and they made me descend several steps, into a small paved courtyard where *café au lait* and a bread called *pistolet*, a traditional breakfast in Brussels, were brought to me. Quite a few hours passed, it seemed; to all my questions on my impending deliverance, vague, I say vague jailers, half "civilians," half policemen, familial, idlers, coarse and bland, responded: "Yes, immediately, you know, they're com'in for ya, don't you doubt it, you'll see...," so that later, towards one o'clock, mashed potatoes and I don't know anymore what half-boiled and roasted meat of veal or lamb, eaten without appetite, I was summoned... to a police van, quite simi-

lar to the "paddy wagons" used in France as the trans-
ports for certain kinds of women to the Prefecture,
that is, metal panels painted yellow and black on the
exterior and giving some view onto the outside. It's in
that way that I traveled through an unfamiliar part of
Brussels, my view wandering out over the hilly
streets full of crowds of poor people, shabby markets,
which climbed from the center of the city to the ancient prison of the Petits-Carmes[43], where I saw myself locked up, not without brutality, but, finally! released from the *cabriolet* and upon exiting the morose
wagon, an ins-pec-tor "laid into" me with his fist, to
say the least, so weighed down was this... bastard!
decorated with silver, and armed with a saber that
never ended, – locked up, I say, under the rubric,
which was transmitted to me on a piece of paper at
the top of which was printed a scale inscribed with
the words "*pro justitia,*" the rubric having been written by the gendarme who handed to me the lock-up
sheet:

"Attempted homicide."

V
The Petits-Carmes

Something like, it appears, the "Depot" in Paris. A
vast paved court, rather long. Frightening fellows in
general. Many Germans, majority Belgians, naturally,
Italians, of course, and too many rather hideous
Frenchmen, alas! I arrive there stunned, timid, as if
still drunk. Besides, well-dressed, I'm a target on the

---

[43]Petits-Carmes, literally "Little-Carmelites" presumably founded
by the Carmelites religious order.

part of my comrades! jeers, sniggers, some looks, which kill me, really. The guard on service, a well-adorned brute, shoves me, while adding Flemish words that I understand by their intonation. He points out to me with his finger a group that's peeling potatoes. Very fatiguing, standing for an hour, that job. The bell rings. It's lunchtime. The walls of the refectory are whitewashed. The tables and benches not clean. The *adjutant*, even more richly decorated than the guard, called sergeant, enormous silver aiguillette and kepi extraordinarily loaded with braids, makes the sign of the cross and with an awful voice:

"*Benedicite,*"

everyone responds, except me who had long ago forgotten this liturgy as well as all the others:

"*Dominus!*"

and the adjutant in response more fiercely than before:

"*Nos et ea quæ sumus sumpturi benedicat dextera Christi.*"

Everyone, including me, this time:

"*Amen.*"

And everyone sits down at tables before mess tins and iron spoons. What swill! Barley with, evidently, horse fat: I recognize it, me, Parisian of the Siege. I taste it with the tip of my tongue: I ate some of it, finally, about one quarter, when the adjutant:

"Gratias, etc."

and everyone returns into the courtyard, which I barely reach when I'm called in to the Director's office.
Through many halls (the Petits-Carmes being, as the
name indicates, an ancient convent), I arrive at length,
accompanied by a guard, his hand on his short sword,
before this potentate who, after having dismissed his
lackey, says to me:

"Please have a seat, Mr. Verlaine."

Finally, a polite word after all that torrent of
humiliations. I looked at the Director, a small man all
mustaches and greying mutton chops, *pince-nez* behind which two piercing eyes, not threatening, sitting
in an armchair. Extraordinarily, he was, at that time,
medaled. Such a man, around 1850-1851, a general of
the national guard, with no end to the torsades[44]! He
holds in his hand a letter addressed to me by Victor
Hugo.

(From the Amigo I had written to the Master
imploring him to intervene on my behalf with some
dear personage.)

The Director: "I have just read some of the
letter that was addressed to you, and I'm surprised,
having received such correspondence, to see you
here. You may read it yourself."

(I later gave the letter to a friend, an English-
man, in Lincolnshire.) It said this:

My dear poet,

*I will pay a visit to your charming wife and
speak with her on your behalf in the name of your
sweet little boy. Have courage and come back soon.*

---

[44]*torsades*: ceremonial or decorative tassels hanging from
epaulettes and hats, for instance, indicative of honors or rank.

– Victor Hugo

The Director, again: "Your mother..." (my poor, good old mother to whom the horrible scene had been related, my mother to whom I have caused so much suffering and who is dead from pneumonia subsequent to a chill contracted while taking care of me when I was completely paralyzed by an illness!), "Your mother has solicited the King's Prosecutor to authorize your being placed in preferential quarters. With this letter in hand here, I take it upon myself to authorize them for you from this moment forward, while waiting for orders in your regards to arrive and which, I have no doubt, will be favorable towards you."

And with a sound of the bell, the guard returned: "Conduct *Monsieur* to the preferential quarters for the accused."

VI

My memory, which would begin to deteriorate if I hadn't put it in good order, and the scandalous lack of attention that I bring to the arrangement of my literary "notes" has made me forget of late quite simply to consign to its place an episode, of the most burning kind, moreover, in my life as a prisoner.

To fill in really quickly this gap, I will very quickly say that as soon as I had left the "depot" of the Petits-Carmes, I was placed, at this same prison, in a cell, by order of the examining magistrate, as if to say at Mazas[45] on the spot. Furniture: a hammock and

---

[45]Mazas: an old prison in Paris that was used from 1850 to 1898.

a blanket, a table, a stool, a washbasin... and a pail. Food: barley patée, on Sundays patée made of crushed peas. Beverage, unlimited water. Particular sign, on the first day, I caught... lice.

With a little ink carefully economized in an inkwell loaned by the administration for epistolary uses only, and conserved, at a price, in an interstice of tiles, I wrote, during the eight days or so of my rather rough custody, with the help of a small piece of wood, the several diabolic recitations that appeared in my book *Jadis et Naguère*, – "Crimen Amoris," which begins like this:

"In a palace, of silk and gold, in Ecbatana"

and four others, of which "Don Juan Duped" which my friend Ernest Raynaud, the excellent poet, has in original manuscript, the paper having served to wrap something, I forget what, from the kitchen, manuscript brought into the world thanks to the barbarous behavior described earlier.

Once a day, in the morning, the various accused, by sections, descended into the "ornamented" paved courtyard, in the middle of a little "garden" in the full yellow bloom of marigolds[46], equipped with their pail... no better or worse than hygienic, which they had to empty at a designated place and rinse before beginning their walk in single file under the watchful eyes of a more or less human guard.

I wrote the following stanzas:

. . . .
They go! And their poor shoes
   Make a popping sound,

---

[46]marigolds: which in French is *"souci"*, which besides marigolds also means care, or worry.

Humiliated,
Pipe in mouth.
Not a word, or it's solitary confinement;
Not a sigh!
It is so hot
One feels one is going to die.[47]

Sundays, hushed voices in a really too ugly chapel, without singing, without a sermon! A sermon is good sometimes, even for blackguards like me!...

It was not, I repeat, until after one week of these joys that I was called into the director's office and that I became a *preferential inmate* as a result of the letter by Victor Hugo, and after my interview with the Director of the prison, as I have recounted previously.

In the meantime, I appeared two or three times before the examining magistrate, and insinuatingly benevolent men, *cosi son tutti,* who had no confession to obtain from me and, by consequence of my frankness at the police station... kept me in a state of imprisonment and had me summoned by the King's Prosecutor, acting on behalf of the criminal court, and held in custody for voluntary shots and woundings that had occurred, etc., etc.

Was the custody any better, for attempt, than that for murder?

No.

VII

Everyone knows what it means to be in preferential

---

[47]They go!... die: from "Other" in *Cellulely.*

quarters. By financial means, one can have his food and his drink (oh how little!) brought in from outside; one enjoys a presentable bed, a chair or even a stool, and other "softness." But captivity, in grave cases like my own, remains as restricted, surveillance as strict, for prisoners as their poverty or the nature of their fault permits in the totally naked horror of the Regulations. It's in this way that the cell I occupied in a building apart was opened only one hour a day for a solitary walk in a courtyard paved but brutally! and sad!

Above the wall in front of my window (I had a window, a real one! equipped, for example, with long and close bars), at the back of the so sad courtyard where frolicked, if I dare to speak like this, my mortal boredom, I saw, it was August, the top of some tall poplar tree, in a neighboring square or boulevard, swinging, with its leaves voluptuously quivering. And I composed, on this subject, these verses which can be found in *Sagesse*.

. . . .
A bird on the tree that one sees
     Sings its plaint.

. . . .
That peaceable sound there
     Comes from the town.

. . . .
What have you done, O you there
     Weeping ceaselessly.
What have you done, O you there

     With your youth?

. . . .
I saw also, spectacle equally melancholic,

keeping guard, up and down, against the wall, on the inside, naturally (and why on the inside?), a chasseur-scout, silk hat with cock feathers, deep green tunic, I believe, grey trousers, who appeared definitely bored out of his mind during the two hours of guard duty. And it made no difference that he was relieved and replaced, his successor did not present more than his predecessor the symptoms of too great an enthusiasm in the accomplishment of those, otherwise, so absurd orders. The good boys seemed to be saying: "What's the point of walking around like this, with a rifle on the shoulder and a sack on the back, to watch over and kill as needed the poor devils so well padlocked and bolted and half-dead already?"

But I had other distractions, the principal one of which consisted in corresponding with my "neighbor," a notary. The *phonetic* alphabet in the true sense, at that time, was largely practiced by us. Do you know it, at least by hearsay? It consists in tapping on a wall one sound for A, or contrariwise – or in a different way tapping one sound for Z, or contrari-wise or in some other way, and so forth. So many small joys *stolen* in this way, tempered by the fear of being caught by the adjutant, a good enough man otherwise and whom the *Game* left only indifferent.

The day of my court hearing came finally.

Risum teneatis.

VIII

It comes back to me, – the new Palace of Justice in Brussels is monumental in a Babel-like way, and I want to believe it.

The old one was hideous in its inconvenience, of an ugliness and even of a leprous poverty, literally. One reached it, I don't even know how anymore, so much do I detest still the two visits that I made there, "out of the blue," by means of the infamous vehicle mentioned earlier; but I can certify that one entered into it ill at ease, through innumerable corridors, over kinds of footbridges, bridges, veritably tiring, between two gendarmes terribly coiffed with busbies that would set the old guard of the first Empire's hair on fire. – Not nasty, for all that, the Belgian gendarmes. You know, doubtless, that they enlisted themselves, contrary to the practice with us, as with the rest of the army, – such that they are all young men still accessible to pity or at least to some compassion for their quasi-citizens. I had experience with this, as one will see, and I dispatch hence to that body, which is not anywise elite over there, but special in a completely fine way, my very cordial *bonjour,* not goodbye, all the same, in spite of the pleasant procedures, of which here is quittance.

In any case, they led me, those excellent cops, with the tall coifs and strong boots, after a probational period in a rather poorly furnished vestibule, into the... nth Chamber (I can't remember the number) of the Correctional Court.

Ugly, narrow, and mangy that room, or rather that hall, formerly whitewashed, at that time completely flaking, cracked, and as if threatening to fall apart. On the front wall (the public officials sitting on wooden benches, equipped only with dossiers of such quantity that someone it seems would have wept to have to put them there), a scabrous Christ hanging who appeared to wear his hair too long and to have been perched in that place to watch the accused

"With a cross expression."

The three counsellors entrusted to take on my case sat in armchairs hidden by their large arms, attired similarly to our French judges, behind a table covered in a solid green cloth, on which lay codes, papers, writing cases, and a central lectern for the President.

They had me sit in front of the tribunal on a simple stool without gendarmes at my sides, my attorney behind me, in a costume almost exactly like that of the attorneys whom Europe envies us for and whom France dispatches, in great masses, to our Chamber of Justice and into power.

"My audience" began. Same ceremony as in France:

"The accused will rise."

"Your full name?"

"Profession?"

"You are accused of having..., etc." and, after interrogation, otherwise short and not too fierce, the traditional:

"Please have a seat."

And as I was obeying, the King's Prosecutor rose.

I can still see that individual, small handlebar mustache, small mutton chops called *"Cambronne,"* one hand in the pocket of his white twill trousers (why not made of canvas?) rolled up casually, like a Hussard, black robe, while his other hand was removing from the top of his small head, the disgraceful heavy toque of his profession and put it on the narrow table, which was also covered in the same décor of a green cloth like that of the tribunal and, like it, loaded with codes, papers, a writing case, and a lectern.

"Gentlemen," he began, while referring to me, "the man whom you have before you is a foreigner..."

And it was comical to hear, in French, that too Belgian accent of some young man just out of Leuven, or Gand, or some other local university.

Then, passing to the facts of the case, and after having deplored that he was practicing civil law and not standing before a military tribunal for which "drunkenness is not an excuse," he condemned me while treating me as a coward (what logic!). "Yes, gentlemen, the assassin," – he forgot that the accusation of murder had been abandoned, "yes, the assassin draws from his pocket a loaded, six-round revolver" (simplistic, if it had not been loaded, what good was it to draw from my pocket? let's be a little reasonable here), "he aims at his victim" (pronounced "victimne"), "two shots leave the gun, one of which strikes the poor wretch." (O Rimbaud, by that time treated comfortably for your boo-boo, which I will lament in any case for the rest of my life for having caused you, all the while wanting to have done worse besides, how you would have laughed, poor friend gone forever, to hear yourself spoken of like that!) "And then, gentlemen, not content with his first crime" (read misdemeanor)...

And the "presenting magistrate" recounts in his own words and in his own manner the scene, otherwise deplorable, and the street, and finally insists that I be given "all the severities provided for by law."

In conformance with his conclusions, in spite of a good pleading by my defense attorney, the tribunal, without having deliberated any longer than required by law, applied to me the maximum sentence, two years imprisonment.

At that moment, and before the public, I maintained a good countenance. But once returned in steel chains, under a bailiff's guard, into the vestibule where the gendarmes waited for me, I burst out crying like a child, so much so that "my guardian angels" began to console me in these terms, word for word:

"It's only for a short while, there's still the appeal, buck up."

And my attorney, having appeared, had me, in effect, sign a document to appeal.

Then, horse whips, coach driver (the prison's), to the Petits-Carmes, *iterum*.

IX

I adore the costumes, and I am wild about the symbols. Also, despite the enormous and so odiously frequent absurdity of five out of six judgments rendered by this, that, and the other Court, I love, in spite of my hatred for bad actions, the good bearing of men of justice (guillotines included, while expecting better).

A black robe worn well, a well-assumed *rabat*, an *epitoge*, in the case of courts of assize, with epaulettes, seduces my mind, if not my person.

And I will always pay homage to them, as I would bear arms for these things, reminder, also, of our divine origin, black then white feathers, aigrettes, black and tricolor plumes, pompoms of various colors, comparative epaulettes, graduated stripes, chevrons, – and simple button (in the case of glorious capitulation!).

As well, I pride myself on an immense respect

for the magistrature, and I do not wish anyone to mis-
understand me or my opinions on that score.

It has, also, – over and above its admirable
discipline! its insignia, stripes, *rabats* which are its
chinstraps (for there is no longer a high collar), – and,
in short, its flag, which is Christ on the cross!...

That's why I accepted, indulgent, without
cursing, the just judgment, for I merited the scaffold,
in fact.

But as I had appealed, it was necessary for
me, having no other choice, to resign myself to this
perspective, still consoling! Eighteen months!!...

And the day of appeal shined, if I dare express
myself in this way.

Shined! Because what beautiful weather, that
day then, what a sun! – Me, a Northerner, I have little
admiration, little love for the sun, it makes me nau-
seous, it makes me dizzy, it blinds me and I absolutely prefer

"Lucid winter"

like our dear, great Stéphane Mallarmé.

Therefore, to write about it judiciously, at one
o'clock, – how could I forget? – in the afternoon, I
was, by the villainous locomotion mentioned previously, conducted once again, by means of the quasi-
military police apparatus of yesteryear, back into the
palace of justice there.

Walls covered with paper: one would have
thought he was in, at that time, the eating room of a
village hotel. No Christ on the wall, – and, truly! that
was better than the caricature in the first instance.

Covered with paper with designs on them.
What motifs? I don't remember. Flowers, hunting

scenes, fishing or galant celebrations? – I don't remember, I tell you, occupied as I was with something
else. Let's see, where were we!

And from the top again, with some variance:

"The convicted will rise."

"Your full name?"

"Profession?"

"You have been convicted in virtue of
article...," etc.

"Please sit down."

I sit down – in spite of an astonishing closing
speech that discharged me by good logic, and mocked
that baby of a prosecutor in the first instance, putting
under his nose this:

*"The maximum penalty was applied to the
convicted and the King's Prosecutor appeals to raise
the maximum sentence. Where is the law,
gentlemen?"*

And notwithstanding an excellent pleading on
the part of my attorney – the same as in the first instance – to whom I send my best sympathies, my
original sentence was confirmed.

X
Mons

This time I was really and truly put away. And
I was admitted to privileged quarters for the convicted. A relative liberty: the doors to the rooms were left
open from six in the morning to eight in the evening,
and each of the prisoners had access to one another. A
group of twenty or so "comrades" of whom several
were French, which didn't flatter me much.

I remained there for about one month and this

was, materially, the happiest period of my captivity. And then, the prison wagon for... Mons.

The prison, cellular also, in the capital of Hainaut, is, I must confess, the prettiest thing possible. Made of pale red brick, almost pink, on the exterior, this monument, this veritable monument, is whitewash white and black as tar on the inside, with sober steel and iron architectures. I expressed the kind of admiration that was caused in me on sight of, O the very first sight of, from that moment on, my "chateau" in my verse, which some readers found amusing, in *Sagesse*, the majority of whose poems, besides, date from then...

> *I have for a long time inhabited the best*
> *of chateaus.*

After descending the train, I went by vehicle, always cellular, and was conducted to that almost friendly prison, where I was received with total simplicity, it must be said; after which I was invited – peremptorily – to take a bath, and quite bizarre clothing was brought to me, consisting of a leather cap with a shape that one could say evoked Louis XI, a jacket, a vest, a pair of trousers made of a material whose name escapes me, greenish, tough, rather similar to very thick repp, very coarse and all said very ugly, a fat neck wrap made of wool, socks and sabots.

Thus attired, I was made to get into the cellule that was assigned to me. Contents, the furniture, – for I had fallen back into the category of ordinary prisoner, while waiting for new procedures to take place to the effect that I would be in preferential quarters again.[48]

My costume was completed by the addition of a blue canvas cowl destined to hide the face of prisoners in their passage through the corridors for walks in the exercise yard, – and by a large black varnished plaque of copper, a little in the shape of a heart, with my number in relief, shining more beautifully than gold even. I had to hang that sign on myself when I went on each walk, from a button on my jacket.

Then the barber of the establishment shaved me in conformance with the rules. I was elegant and pretty, I assure you.

But let's get back to the furniture of the cellule.

A bed-table that one should not deploy and *make* except in the evening, just before going to bed. A wooden bench attached to the wall, a washbasin and a sort of nook in the wall for private usages. A little crucifix in copper, which I would later become familiar with, completed this scant luxury.

O that crucifix!

XI

That crucifix in my first cellule at Mons wouldn't necessarily be the very same one that I interacted with, but a crucifix in many ways similar to all others that grace all locales of the vast penitentiary.

But let's get back to the furnishings. I omitted

---

[48]preferential quarters: the French word is *pistole*, which is assumed to be metonymical for Spanish coins of the same name, with the understanding that if one had pistoles (the coins) one could purchase a place in the pistole (preferential quarters).

a piece, and not the least important. I want to speak of the adjutant or head guard of the wing where I was then (the subaltern guards had the title of sergeant, as I already mentioned). This adjutant, I say, wasn't kindly disposed towards me, and if he visited me often, it wasn't in order to see me, but really and truly to inspect me. And innumerable observations ensued, as well as threats of solitary confinement, for something as minor as a speck of dust, a bad fold in the folded blanket on my bed-table when the bed had been turned into a table, even something, in his mind, irregular in my person, such as my collar wrap not in conformance with the regulations, a loose button on my jacket, etc. How he made me suffer, that animal, with his ferocious minutia! Otherwise, a hell of good guy and who would necessarily grow human a little later, with respect to me, at least.

The food? Eh, my goodness, always some soup... with barley, and on Sundays pea purée, supply bread, water as much as I wanted.

Sundays, mass, vespers, and salutations sung by the detainees. Harmonium played by a woman from the city, sermons well delivered by the almoner, a charming man of whom I have retained the best and most grateful memory.

The chapel, very extraordinary: contrary to the arrangement in most cellular prisons, the altar and its accessories are located in the middle, naturally, of the *boxes* intended for the "faithful," but quite elevated on a platform, at four corners of which stand the guards charged with ensuring good conduct and respect for the Holy Place...

It's the same that my verses in *Parallèlement* make allusion to.

. . . .
See the salutations light up
     From the bottom of a hole.

The exercise yards in prison form a wheel whose central rotunda is the hub from which radiate, like a V, a dozen walls hemming in as many small, rather gloomy, gardens, where there is a V in the masonry. A guard is stationed inside the rotunda and gives a light to the prisoners, who have one hour to smoke a pipe and pace about like wolves, each one in his own exercise yard. After which, return to the cellules, in indian file, cowls on head, – and that's it until tomorrow, at the same hour.

But at the end of eight or ten days of this regimen, which was not so agreeable, but so comfortable and sufficient, fundamentally! I was called to the Director's office, ever a charming man, growing grey in the hair already, very benevolent and with whom I became friendly from the first moment.

What luck! it had to do with my being placed in preferential quarters.

I was led into another building structure. My new cellule, a bit larger than the other, but furnished even, except for a bed, which was good, large, and allowing for the freedom of being able to stretch finally, pleased me from the start.

It was however but only barely comfortable. And above all that, lighting, which was otherwise sufficient, filtering through the horizontal bars, but entering from too high up and barring, – at the risk of repeating myself, – the horizon. But what happiness at last to sleep in a proper bed! And what felicity it was to lie in this room, seemingly more modest than, formerly alas! that old modest, but commodious, conjugal room, with its bed "in the middle."

One must learn to be content with little things, especially in prison, and as every thought of woman was forbidden to me perforce, it was perforce therefore that I had to resign myself. Which I did.

I asked for books. I was permitted to have a complete library. Dictionaries, classics, a copy of Shakespeare in English, which I read in its entirety (I had a lot of time, go figure!). Precious notes by Johnson and all the English, German, and other commentators, helped me to understand well the immense poet, who nevertheless never allowed me to forget Racine any more than Fénelon nor La Fontaine, not to mention Corneille and Victor Hugo, Lamartine and Musset. And no journals!

These diversions were not my only ones, however.

I invented a game.

It consisted in chewing up paper into two little balls, supposing two adversaries, A and B, launching these projectiles alternatively in the direction of a target that was the judas of the cellule and keeping score faithfully.

Double pleasure. At first, to win or to lose. Whatever A detested in B, B stuck it to him again so well! Then there was the fear of the adjutant or sergeant passing by. Or, even! the Director himself.

To tell the truth, I feared the Director the least.

XII

Jesus, you acted as you did in order to win me over?

Ah!

One morning, the Director himself entered my cellule.

"My poor friend," he said to me, "I bear bad news. Stiff upper lip. Read!"

It was a sheet of stamped paper, the copy of a judgment of separation of person and property, so merited all the same (of person! and perhaps also of property?), but hard under the circumstances! what the civil court of the Seine ascribed to me. I broke down in tears on my poor back on my poor bed.

A handshake and a pat on the shoulder by the Director infused in me, nonetheless, a little courage, – and, one or two hours after this scene, lo and behold I asked my "sergeant" to request that the Almoner come and speak with me.

This latter came and I asked for the catechism. He immediately gave me the catechism of persever-ance by Monseigneur Gaume.[49]

I'm a man of letters, I appreciate correction, subtlety, the complete cuisine of style, as by right and duty. Even these corrections, these subtleties, I took them, I sniffed at them, if you will. And I'm horrified by all written platitudes.

But, in spite of an actually deplorable art of writing and syntax that had barely any life to it, Mon-seigneur Gaume was for me, oozing with pride, the apostle of syntax and Parisian stupidity.

XIII

The rather mediocre proofs evidenced by Monseigneur Gaume in favor of the existence of God

---

[49]*Catéchisme de persévérance:* written by Monseigneur Jean-Joseph Gaume.

and of the immortality of the soul pleased me little
and didn't convert me at all, I confess, despite the ef-
forts by the almoner to corroborate them by his better
and more heartfelt commentaries.

It's then that this latter had a great idea and
said to me: "Skip the chapters and pass immediately
to the sacrament of the Eucharist."

And I read a hundred pages consecrated by the
good prelate to the sacrament of the Eucharist.

I cannot say whether these pages constitute a
work of art. I doubt it even. But, the spiritual condition wherein I found myself, the profound boredom to
which I had descended, in spite of all good considerations and of a relatively happy life that these considerations had given me, and the despair of not being
free and, also, the shame so to speak of finding myself there, determined in me, one certain early morning of June, after that bitter-sweet night passed medi-
tating on the real Presence and on the innumerable
multiplicity of hosts represented in the Holy Gospels
by the multiplication of loaves and fish, – all that, I
say, determined in me an unprecedented revolution –
really!

For several days there was, hanging from the
wall of my cellule, under the little crucifix made of
copper, similar to what was mentioned earlier, a
rather frightening lithographic image, as well, of the
Sacred Heart: a long equine head of Christ, a large
emaciated bust under generous folds of clothing, with
tapered hands showing his heart

That radiates and that bleeds

as I needed to write a little later in *Sagesse*.

I don't know what or Who lifted me suddenly,

pulled me out of bed, with no time to put on my clothes, and prostrated me with tears, with sobs, at the feet of the Crucifix and the supererogatory, evocative image of the strangest but in my eyes most sublime devotion of modern times of the Catholic church.

At the very hour of rising, two hours or less perhaps after this veritable small (or great?) moral miracle, I got up again, and I went about, according to regulations, attending to my house work (make the bed, sweep the room...) when the dayshift guard entered and addressed me with this traditional phrase: "How's it going?"

I responded to him immediately:

"Tell the Almoner to come."

This latter entered my cellule several minutes later. I told him of my "conversion."

It was a serious one. I believed, I saw, it seemed to me that I knew, I was enlightened. I would have gone off to martyrdom for good, – and I had immense contrition evidently proportional to the greatness of the Offended, but doubtless, in light of my present examination, strongly exaggerated.

Besides, one is often proud when one compares oneself.

And I am like most men.

The almoner, a man of prison experience and for sure habituated to these sorts of conversion, true or false, but, I am convinced, persuaded by my sincerity, nonetheless calmed me down, after having congratulated me on the grace received, then, because, in my probable indiscretion and imprudence as a neophyte of just yesterday, literally, being a complete miscreant and total sinner, I asked him, I implored him, to confess me immediately, for fear that I might die impenitent, I said. He responded to me, smiling a little:

"Have no fear. You are no longer impenitent, it's me who assures you of it. As for absolution and even the simple benediction, please wait a few days still; God is patient, and he will want you to acquire some credit even, he who waits for his due after so long a time, isn't that right?

"And I'll see you again very, very soon, today even."

XIV

And the worthy, very worthy man of God, left me alone.

I obeyed his system and resigned myself, praying.

Praying, through my tears, through my smiles, like a child, like a redeemed criminal, praying, O, on both knees, with both hands, with all my heart, with all my soul, with all my strength, according to my resuscitated catechism!

How much I reflected on the essence and the evolution even of the thing that operated on me! Why, how?

And I had a sufficiency of these ardors, a sufficiency of these, how might one call it in our odious times, dispositions! How good I was, how simple and small!

And ignorant!

"*Domine, noverim te!*"[50]

What candor of a choir boy, what kindness of an old man, – and young! at that time, a converted

---

[50]*Domine, noverim te!*: Latin for "God, I should know you," or "God, let me know you."

sinner, a proud man humbling himself, a violent man become a lamb!

I abdicated, from that moment forward, all reading materials as "profane," Shakespeare, among others, already read and re-read in the original with access to a dictionary and finally remembered by heart, so to speak. And I dove into works by de Maistre[51], works more particular than those by August Nicolas[52]...

I had nevertheless some timid objections that the almoner refuted more or less adroitly, admirably for me at that epoch.

"But animals, after death?... There is no mention of them in the sacred books."

"My dear friend, if the sacred books don't speak of them any more than of the daughters of Adam, for example, it's because it's superfluous. Besides, God, being infinite kindness, didn't create the beasts except for their own good as well as our own."

"But eternal hell?"

"God is infinite justice and if he punishes for eternity he has his reasons for it, superior reasons before which our unique right is to submit to them even while not understanding them. Because, in effect, eternal punishments are a kind of mystery... But no, because the Dogma does not place them at that level."

And so forth.

The great day, so anticipated, so impatiently desired, of confession, finally arrived...

It was long, infinitely detailed, this confes-

---

[51]de Maistre: Joseph-Marie de Maistre (1753-1821), a French-speaking Savoyard writer, philosopher, diplomat.

[52]August Nicholas, (1807-1888) a French Roman Catholic writer of apologetics.

sion, my first since that of the renewal of my first communion. Sensual faults, principally, faults of anger, faults of intemperance, also numerous, these, faults of small lies, of vague and unconscious deceits, sensual faults, I insist...

The priest, from time to time, helped me in the confessions, always a little painful in such cases, given the bizarre neophyte that I was.

Among other questions, he put to me, this priest, in a calm and nowise surprising nor surprised tone:

"You have never *been* with animals, right?"

XV

After having answered, "no!" not without stupefaction at the interrogation put to me, I received on a humble and contrite forehead, even after my very honest and conscientious, I assure you, confession, the benediction, but not yet the absolution so coveted.

And while waiting for this latter, I resumed, on my spiritual director's advice, my work, various readings, and principally my verse.

From that epoch dates more or less all of *Sagesse*:

My God said to me...

among other poems that have been generally applauded.

My readings, from this epoch forward, in addition to intense theologies, went back to the English or Latin, not only the Fathers, Saint Augustine, that sublime *congener*, whom I was or believed myself to be the vile successor of, but also, among the profane and classic authors, Virgil, and all his *Eclogues*, all the *Georgics*, a large part of the *Aeneid* were included.

The good director of the prison and the excellent almoner crammed with me almost every day.

Finally, I had a guard, who, wishing to leave "the box," as he called it, "completed his instruction" in view of going elsewhere, asked me one fine day to give him French lessons. And then look at us, me dictating, him writing in his large handwriting, at first grammar examples,

Etes-vous Madame de Genlis? etc.

and, when real progress was attained, with passages carefully chosen from the *Adventures of the Young Telemachus* by M. de Salignac-Fénelon, archbishop of Cambrai.

In exchange for these lessons, the good fellow procured for me sweet things, local journals, pastries, chocolate, sometimes the drop and very often, – O joy, O recognition! – some chew (now, chew was forbidden) and the difficulty in hiding traces of it, after usage was complete, made it more delicious still.

What ruses, what tricks

for, at the moment of each expectoration in the little basin destined for my ablutions, to run a thin and as silent as possible trickle of water, to the effect of diluting and making disappear through the metal grate the elimination of proof of the terrible offense.

Thursdays and Sundays, my mother, in possession each time of a permission from the King's

Prosecutor, came to see me. O how painful (and sweet!) these visits through two wire meshes about one meter apart. No means to embrace save by a sign of the hand to the lips, not to speak of spies behind the door, right against it, equipped with a judas whence one is observed at leisure. No matter! my good mother drew from her pocket a *Figaro* purchased at the train station, the said *Figaro* arranged, or rather elongated by twisting, in the form of a very fine fencing foil, and passed through the two wire meshes. What emotions, you can judge for yourselves! and what emotions to unfurl and then to read this journal which, if I had been caught with it in my hands would have earned me solitary confinement, the privation of visits, the suppression of privileged quarters, and other inconveniences!

And a thousand other minute joys and small miseries to which, thanks to my new ideas, I resigned myself, and finished by habituating myself, Christianly! when the dawn of the great day when I should "receive my Savior" arose...

I composed on the subject of Communion some verses that I'm told were good both in *Sagesse*, my book of a neophyte, if I dare to qualify it thus, as in subsequent volumes, more appeased but not less sincere, *Amour*, *Bonheur*, and my most recent, *Intimate Liturgies*:

> *... Let go of indecisive ignorance,*
> . . . .
> . . . .
> *To suffer and die a wicked death.*

(I don't speak, of course, of *Parallèlement*, wherein I feign to receive communion instead with

the Devil.) I cannot, as I could not then, write the poems any better, poems in which I have the immense
sensation of freshness, renunciation, resignation, experienced on that unforgettable day of the Assumption, 1874.

From that day forward, my captivity which
was supposed to last until January 16, 1875, appeared
short to me, and if it hadn't been for my mother, I
would say too short!

XVI

Yes, from that day forward, I was, it's appropriate to say it, "like no one." No one could have in-
sulted me whom I would not have pardoned, at least
made perceive – not as I would today, make feel, –
his wrong, nobody could have looked at me whom I
wouldn't have responded to with an interior prayer
for the salvation of his soul and this vow thought in
Latin: "*Vade retro.*"

O yes! I was, from that Assumption until the
day of my literal and material, if not physical, "liberation," happy.

Yes!

Think about it: to feel innocent, to believe
oneself innocent, at least to believe, and beyond that,
to know it. *Innocent*, think about it!

And I sailed in that kind of skiff, in that
"boat" as the filthy contemporary spirit would blas-
pheme it, – until January sixteenth, of eighty-five, –
like a Don Quixote, more foolish still, en route... for
other windmills.

I sailed in this way towards my "liberation,"
which would take place on that humid day of January.

The night before, my watch was returned to me (I had one and even many, before this time and even since), my wallet, furnished with several banknotes, which I was equally accustomed to carry, my shirt with its false collar, and some loose-fitting elegant clothes.

With Mama accompanying me, after the release from prison, and shaking hands with the office employees, and also, previously, with the almoner, the director, and the guards, I exited from that nearly padded "box,", for the Mons train station finally! – between Mama and me, two gendarmes with fur hats on and clean-shaven faces.

And lo and behold there we were, departed for France where, as is the custom, and rightly! the gendarmerie, with their hats askew as you know, took *us* off the hands of the young *maréchausée*, bearded Κατα χεφαλην mentioned previously.

Our orderly national army received us (I say and repeat "*us*", because there were several liberated Frenchmen, murderers, thieves, and me, expulsed) without great cordiality. Even, insofar as I was concerned, after my having declined[53] (why not conjugated?) my last name, first name, the particulars of my case, I obtained from the sergeant, my compatriot, a reception that was so, wasn't it? infuriating, encouraging, "encore ageant."[54]

"And whatever you do, don't come back."

"No, my sergeant..."

Douai! My mother who was, to the end, so de-

---

[53]declined: In the sense of having "spelled out", but with a subsequent pun on grammatical declination.

[54]*encore ageant*: a play on words that does not translate well into English. Essentially it means "encouraging."

voted to me, so good, – so clement! accompanied me, as I have related above. Douai! Holy city! where Desbordes-Valmore was born in the shadow of that other Notre-Dame, which it has always remembered amidst so many Parisian troubles and preoccupations, – and how many *stages*, the poor woman! – Douai and your tender carillon and canal.

> – *Boatman, says Lisette.....*
> – *Turlututu, Gayant[55] who farts,*
> *Turlututu, by the hole in your arse!*

Douai, hello!

XVII

In V***.[56] – Pleasant city in the extreme, almost Vosgeoise, where I was interned on charges of intimidation against my mother, a crime according to the penal Code, punishable by death, – hand lopped off, barefoot... O Mama!

O Mama, indeed! Pardon me for saying this:

"If you don't come back, I'm going to kill MYSELF!"

Some dreadful Belgians who had monopolized your trust, didn't denounce me, after my filing a complaint, before the public prosecutor G***, in V***, for violation of domestic privacy by the afore-

---

[55]Gayant: a giant symbolizing the city of Douai, since the XIVth century.

[56]V***: Vouziers, where the poet was imprisoned for one month in 1885 for having been accused of intimidating and threatening to strangle, or strangling, or stabbing (depending on whose testimony one reads) his mother.

said Belgians, domicile given, after several combustions[57] in divers places, at C***, near A***, department of the Ardennes[58].

So much so that one day I received a subpoena and, eight days later, appeared before the tribunal of first instance with jurisdiction!

The way, – shall I call it a Calvary? no! – was charming. A married woman and her husband and me, plus a dog that barked after the crows perched on the highest branches, we were bumped about in what one vulgarly calls a bum-slapper and which commonly

On the boulevard de Gand,

is called a *buggy*.

The *Golden Lion*, – The Golden Lion of the region received us, horse and all. Then we were at Court, that husband and his lady being my witnesses for the defense.

The prettiest trinity of judges that I have ever seen in my delinquent and criminal sort of life.

The president was named Adam. His assessor on the right was named Marie. I forget, – and I ask his pardon, the name of the other assessor who, by a rogatory dispensation, had served me as examining magistrate.

But I remember, O and how! the name of the public prosecutor:

"G***."

---

[57]combustions: from "*incendies*" in French, which figuratively means explosion of violent feelings.

[58]C*** near A***: Coulomnes, between Mazagran and Attigny, in the Ardennes.

I had besides composed verses about him for a volume, qualified as *Invectives*, to be published by my natural enemy, Léon Vanier, 19, quai Saint-Michel.

But let's enter into the Palace of Justice of this miniscule sub-prefecture, and admire the superb architectural nullity of it, *rara avis* in that period of pretensions of every sort.

Let's admire also no less the nullity of this monsieur G***, public prosecutor, radical, zealous, even though I'm told clerical, Catholic, even though he appeared a Free-Thinker, and in some ways my muse... of mahogany.

Judge for yourself.

The arch-known furniture of, it does not matter which, court: oak, somber wallpaper, curtains with the same nuance and three men in black robes and white *rabats*. On the left, a table with the prosecutor behind it, same costume as above plus a cap with golden braids generally on the head, in back, proudly.

The hearing began with trifles, vagabonds, poachers, small thieves, etc. When my case came up, a kind of silence fell among the rather numerous audience that day. I was a kind of respected gentleman in the region, over and above the rather detestable reputation I had: one of Rais[59] bred with several Edgar Allen Poes who would have spiced up their rum and their situation with absinthe and Picon[60]: such was I in the imagination of many of my neighbors from the provinces who had hastened to town to see me, "the

---

[59]Rais: Gilles de Rais, the medieval marshal and monster of France. See *The Trial of Gilles de Rais*, by Georges Bataille, published by Amok Books, 1990, for details.

[60]Picon: a caramel-colored flavored bitter, that usually accompanies beer.

Parisian," judged.

The interrogation proceeded as they all do with those formalities. But the requisition lacked what one might call moderation. For all anyone could tell, I would have been a Herod mixed with a Heliogabalus targeted by the enormous epithets launched thick and fast from the lips of that G*** with whom the bees of Hymettos[61] have never, I fear, had anything to do: the "most infamous of men, the scourge of the country, come to dishonor our countryside." (This took place in the Ardennes and this G*** was from Auvergne.) "I do not know how to qualify this individual and I give up trying to find the words that express all my horror; I will pick it up again, in any case, a bit later during this case of relative unimportance." (Come on now, darling!) such were some of the flowers from his bouquet... In truth, reasonable arguments, no question. And he concluded with the maximum there is – read the codes! – death. The court applied the minimum.

I cannot here nor could I nowise ever thank these gentlemen enough, for what it's worth, nor even perhaps blame them given I was innocent, entangled, as it happened, by more plausible false witnesses. At least I must recognize that they invested themselves, as the saying goes, in this case. Besides, their goodwill, – and their Preambles – "Considering the excellent attitude of the accused during the hearing," finally the benefit of attenuating circumstances that were granted, – all that lessened the idea of prison time to be done again and I am grateful to them for their quittance.

The prison of V*** is quite small: the bars are

---

[61]Hymettos: a mountain range near Athens, Greece, renowned for its thyme honey.

made of wood and painted black. One plays *bouchon*
with the head guard. One does not stay there long, a
month precisely with an additional day added, I believe, when the punishment must be prolonged. There
was, when I was there, a familiar crow, raucous enemy of the scant melodious cats of the establishment,
who, as a result of a series of incongruities in tubs
where the lye flowed, was killed with a shot of a car-
bine by the "boss," and made an excellent broth. I
have recounted the story in detail in my "Memories of
a widower."

In this so good-natured prison I was responsi-
ble for keeping house, dusting, sweeping. Regarding
which, the head guard one day told me that I had done
"a poor work" – the man was a Northerner, – and he
added that I was a much better writer than painter.

(It may be worth mentioning here that I had
acquired by now in the country the reputation of a
"writer.")

I was also asked in the evenings to recite in
the dormitory the *Pater Noster* and the *Ave Marie*, –
and it seemed that I acquitted myself of this charge
much better than my predecessor. Good gracious!
And without much effort really.

An almoner come from Falaise, a neighboring
village that figures in the *Debacle* by Émile Zola, and
who had been a missionary in China, buried alive,
gave us mass on Sundays. His hebdomadal sermon,
full of anecdotes and very pleasant, in that pretty, almost English accent, of the Ardennes, concluded with
a handshake through the bars, made of wood like the
others, with the three or four prisoners that we were.

That lasted one month, at the end of which my
fine (500 francs!) was paid, and I exited in the company of the head guard with whom I drank several

bottles of a certain local wine from Voucq, which is all I have to say about it, in a tavern next door, which was called *The Good Corner* and which merited that denomination.

XVIII

Now, from the old *Chat Noir*, today the *Mirliton*, – transitions! – I exited, one early evening, leaving behind me the delightful Salis[62] and the then *persona grata* Léon Bloy, tiger of the good God, and cat of the good devil, and Marie Krysinka, and so many other loveable monsters, after several extremely prolonged libations? no! well maybe.

I left them then these delightful individuals, and I wended, living in the vicinity of the Bastille, past a station of fiacres not far away, in order to return to my, as yet filial, domicile...

But what the devil got into me? I wanted to refresh the other drinks with ONE last absinthe.

An error in the accounting, after a series of absorptions, caused an outburst, and I felt the need to demand – a lot and very loudly! – my rights.

And I called a keeper of the peace who put me immediately in my place – and not too gently.

Checked in there, and the sub-sergeant of police, or his superior, made me hand over my tie, my pipe, – and my wallet.

I didn't sleep, – my companion was a drunkard who made pee-pee and caca all the time in the internal place for these necessities.

---

[62]Salis: Rodolphe Salis, founder of the Chat Noir, a celebrated cabaret in Montmartre. It was the first cabaret (tavern) to install a piano (unless it wasn't: see *Ten Years a Bohemian* by Goudeau).

But in the morning, at nine o'clock, the "sarges" who had spent the night passing water to us in a tin goblet, the same one, and telling us:

"If that's all you had drunk, you wouldn't 'be here.'"

They freed us.

And, at nine o'clock (about twelve hours of insomnia and how!), I was called by name preceded by Monsieur, to the office of the police commissioner (whose name however escapes me even though he is rather known in these parts), on rue Bochard-de-Saron.

This "magistrate" said nothing to me, – other than my name inscribed on a register and from a receipt given to the agent who had arrested me the night before.

Finally, I escaped from those funny hands there.

Forever?

XIX
Conclusion

Last November I purchased my ticket at the *gare du Nord*[63] for Holland with plans to attend some conferences in La Hague, Leiden and Amsterdam, where I had been invited by several groups of artists, literary types, and students. The trip passed peacefully, all the more so by grace of an unexpected windfall the day before, so that I was able to procure myself a compartment all to myself on the train. Since I have grown sickly, I adore my comforts even though ac-

---

[63]*gare du Nord*: the train station in Paris that serves the region and countries north of Paris.

customed to life's harshnesses now.

I crossed that French region of the Nord, so sad and monotonous, apart from some landscapes, charming near Chantilly, somber in the vicinities of Saint-Quentin and farther, which Alexander I of Russia found *ugly par excellence* with such good reason! I was given then to revisiting in my mind, as if by bird's flight, that's nearly the expression, Belgium previously inhabited, as a child, in the previously French zone of the septentrional Ardennes, named today Belgian Luxembourg, as a man, and much later, all over and in different fashions. Among other materialized memories were, at Mons, the apparition of the

> "... *Chateau that shines all red and sleeps all white.*"[64]

I wish to speak about the cellular prison, which I had never seen so well from without. It's situated at the extremity of the city, assuming the form of a wheel embedded in four walls constituting a rectangle, the whole of it terminated by the chapel's polygonal dome. The door at the entrance lined with grey stone has an artistic turn to it and plays at the gothic style quite well. The patina, perhaps due to the passing of time and distance, appeared to me then, as moreover evoked in the verse that I just quoted a fragment of, blood red; but those bricks that appeared to me thus previously, when viewed up close and a few years after their first employment, were pale pink almost.

Moreover, with my mind on my future conferences and ruminating rhythms, metrics, rhymes, and

---

[64]Chateau...: From *Amour, a* book of poetry by Verlaine.

all the trouble that accompanies those sorts of "talks" on contemporary French and Franco-Belgic poetry, I passed by, without too much emotion invested in it, that severe asylum where, nine years earlier, I had suffered so much and enjoyed so much.

I arrive there, I practice my occasional profession as orator or rather lecturer much better than worse and obtain from an indulgent public all the success I can hope for. I savor for several too brief days, the calm cordiality, the fine and thoughtful good-naturedness of my new friends, their applause, their praises after each session, on the days following and in three quarters of the literary and artistic journals of that country. I admire that strange country, all greenery and all water, those towns with traditional architecture – and I catch again, almost alas! the train for Paris. I pass by Mons again and see it once more,

"... Chateau that shines all red and sleeps all white."

And this time I'm taken back in time:

The path I had just taken as a literal little prince, a veritable baron of finance, on padded cushions, surrounded by all possible comforts and the object of all regards on the part of the employees of every grade, I endured it in the past, in a cellular wagon, and then to step down from a paddy wagon into a penitentiary courtyard between the prison guards and the gendarmes as escort.

There, I moaned at first, blasphemed, for having such vile, such stupid, and sometimes such hateful regrets – then, as I've recounted several pages above, came the conversion – and the happiness over the course of a perseverance of several years. The slack-

ening that followed little by little, then new descents...
Irremediable?

Maybe not, for God is merciful and has always sent me unhappiness, ruin in the most upsetting
circumstances really, really! deceptions, betrayals by
the next scandalized person: a lady? also? Maybe not,
but this cowardice, that softness, that stubbornness
once again in impenitence, instinctive stubbornness,
practically bestial...

A false welcome waited for me in Paris:
hypocrisy, dishonesty, finally theft, clever and wily,
because plausible, of several banknotes that I brought
with me. My exasperation on the subject earned me
two days later a disagreement that could have turned
worse, if it weren't for my moderation before the giv-
en situation. A very violent quarrel on my stairway
made the concierge come, who called the agents of
police. These latter, taking my anger and his vehe-
mence as a result of too prolonged sessions at taverns,
threw me, O for an hour or two... in the slammer not
without useless brutality.

Shall l describe for you again these grotesque
police scenes that are, all said and done, even more
abominable than stupid? Isn't there enough of this
type of disgusting behavior. I finish by being unable
to go on any longer as a result of painful evocations...

Me, the triumphant from over there, the ac-
claimed, the cherished foreigner, on the day after my
return, in the slammer! and not even drunk!

O gentlemen of the French police, what a
"blunder," to speak the language that suits you and
that pleases you; run then in haste after the lawbreak-
ers if you dare, and leave the poets be. They don't re-
gard you, in both senses of the word.

But it's true that nobody is a prophet in their

own country.

But, also! O the catechism of Monseigneur Gaume, O unable to read him again, not willing, perhaps, to re-read him – and not budging this time!

God, nevertheless, is merciful and hope is a theological virtue that he dispenses more willingly:

Lord, have pity on us.